Alexander Pope

Alexander Pope

by

George S. Fraser

Reader in Poetry
University of Leicester

Routledge & Kegan Paul
London, Henley and Boston

First published in 1978
by Routledge & Kegan Paul Ltd
39 Store Street,
London WC1E 7DD,
Broadway House,
Newtown Road,
Henley-on-Thames,
Oxon RG9 1EN and
9 Park Street,
Boston, Mass. 02108, USA
Set in 11 on 12 Bembo
and printed in Great Britain by
Ebenezer Baylis and Son Ltd,
The Trinity Press, Worcester, and London
© *George S. Fraser, 1978*

British Library Cataloguing in Publication Data

Fraser, George Sutherland

Alexander Pope.
1. Pope, Alexander – Criticism and interpretation
821'.5   PR3634   78-40731

ISBN 0 7100 8990 2

Contents

Preface

I would like first of all to thank my publishers for their patience in waiting for this text. Shortly after agreeing to write it, I was struck, for the first time in my life, with what might well have been a mortal combination of serious physical illnesses. I survived, and my convalescence was rapid, but when I set myself to write a first draft I realised that it was not up to my standards. The growing pressure of university teaching in recent years (and the special responsibilities of a senior teacher, much concerned with supervising research) made it difficult to find time to re-write.

I have found time at last. What I have done here, if not ideal, is at least now more or less what I was setting out to do, and I hope, in its plain way, may tempt many readers to look at a great poet from whom they might get much pleasure.

I write as a lover of poetry (and a lover of the eighteenth century) but not as a scholar in the work of this poet or this period. I will be happy if I can persuade others to share my own amateur enjoyment. I owe much to the conversation of colleagues who are true scholars of the period, my revered former chief, A. R. Humphreys, our present Head of Department, J. S. Cunningham, who has written brilliantly on *The Rape of the Lock*, and my combative neighbour across the corridor, in Leicester, W. H. Myers, very much a Dryden rather than a Pope man. To all, thanks.

GSF

Introduction

Pope, as the first chapter here explains, was born shortly before the abdication of King James II, in a violent and bigoted period of English history, when Great Britain was a minor power and France, both by her culture and her arms, dominated Europe. It was a time of change, but, as the brief sketch of his life – whose main achievement was his poetry and its main drama his friendships and enemies, many of them among the great – in Chapter 2 makes clear, both his ill-health and his religion (Roman Catholicism) prevented him from taking any active part (except, very indirectly, in later life as a satirist). The rest of this book follows his work: the first youthful collected *Works* of 1717; the version of Homer, about ten years' work begun around 1715; the poem on natural religion, *An Essay on Man*, Pope's most popular production; and his *Moral Essays* or *Epistles to Several Persons* in which the lessons of *An Essay on Man* are applied to specific moral questions; and finally to two kinds of satire, the ferocious mock-epic, *The Dunciad*, and the much gayer *Imitations of Horace*.

One argument of this book is that it is a mistake to think of Pope as primarily a satirist; another is that, always at ease in aristocratic company, in some ways he is more like a survivor from the Restoration than a precursor, like his enemy Addison, of the new middle-class morality. Critically, the emphasis is on his acute sensibility and the variety of his talent. It is argued that he is not mainly a satirist and that his satires themselves, because they indulge both his admirations and his hatreds so freely, and therefore lack coolness, are perhaps often great poems (*Epistle to Dr Arbuthnot* is a great autobiographical poem) rather than great satires of a conventional kind. Pope's poems are so personal that throughout the critical chapters some further discussion of his life and character has seemed necessary. The last chapter discusses the very contrasting views of his gifts as a poet taken by other poets and by some notable critics from his own time till today and, without attempting to settle a great critical controversy, indicates my broadly favourable verdict.

1

Pope: A Poet between Two Ages

Alexander Pope was born in May 1688 (he died, about ten days after his birthday, in May 1744), in the last few months of the reign of James II. He was born late in the second marriage of a prosperous London linen merchant, who, perhaps influenced by commercial trips to Portugal, had become converted to Roman Catholicism. His elder half-sister, Mrs Rackett, always disliked little Alexander and thought him a 'maddish' boy.

Pope's father, as the son of a clergyman, could just rank as a gentleman. But when, on the accession of William and Mary, Roman Catholics had to settle out of London, the elder Alexander, on retiring to a small farm in Windsor Forest, soon made friends not only among the Romanist country gentry but, because of his son's precocious poetic talent and lively ways, with a staunch Protestant Whig like Sir William Trumbull, who had held high office under William. Pope's father was given plenty of time to move and settle, for William, though a devout Calvinist, was not a persecutor. Pope adhered loyally throughout his life to the religion of his parents but his Catholicism was of a liberal, humanist, Erasmian kind, and his great poem on natural religion, *An Essay on Man*, appealed not only to Protestants and Catholics but even to Muslims. Pope was, unlike his friend Bolingbroke, no deist; but his Christianity was latitudinarian and tolerant.

Pope, thus, has little or nothing to say about original sin, about grace or the atonement, or, except in *The Messiah*, where he skilfully blends Virgil and Isaiah, about the incarnation. He learned, as a poet, to avoid the mysteries. He was impressed, however, by Newton:

Nature, and Nature's Laws, lay hid in Night.
God said, *Let Newton be!* and All was *Light*,

and believed with complete sincerity both that a divine intelligence has

1

shaped a harmonious universe and that the seeds of self-love, which God has planted in us to make us active beings, will find fulfilment, and we shall find the happiness at which we all aim, only in social benevolence. The young Pope delighted not only in the potential goodness of men but (he had a sharp eye for colour and his hobby was painting) in the colours and beauty of outward nature, which in the early *Pastorals* and the slightly later and richer *Windsor Forest* he paints with a Keatsian vividness. When Pope speaks of Nature, however, as he often does, he is not thinking like Wordsworth of 'something far more deeply interfused' but of the spontaneous creative power of a great poet like Homer, as Pope describes him in his first major poem *An Essay on Criticism*, and of the necessity in poetry of truth to common life and feeling. Even though, in wit, affection, or anger he is the most socially observant of all our great poets, his passages of very high eloquence are largely reserved for moments when he is carried away by his sense of the power of poetry itself.

Pope is sublime at such moments, just as he has true pathos when he speaks of the skill and friendship of his physician, Dr Arbuthnot, and of the diversion of poetry, as things that help him through 'that long Disease, my life'. Though Pope is a most accomplished satirist, and now chiefly famous for his satire, I think he became a satirist almost by accident, because of the extreme sensibility of a life-long invalid to personal attack: personal resentment too often robs his satire of what Saintsbury, speaking of his great predecessor Dryden, calls 'coolness at the centre'. He differs from Dryden, moreover, in having a haunting sense of beauty:

As one by one, at dread Medea's strain,
The sick'ning stars fade off th'ethereal plain;
As Argus' eyes, by Hermes' wand opprest,
Clos'd one by one to everlasting rest . . .

Lo! where Maeotis sleeps, and hardly flows
The freezing Tanais thro' a waste of snows . . .

He lifts the Tube, and levels with his Eye;
Strait a short Thunder breaks the frozen Sky.
Oft, as in Airy Rings they skim the Heath,
The clam'rous Lapwings feel the Leaden Death:
Oft as the mounting Larks their Notes prepare,
They fall, and leave their little lives in Air . . .

Our plenteous Streams a various Race supply;
The bright-ey'd Perch with Fins of *Tyrian* Dye,
The silver Eel, in shining Volumes roll'd,
The yellow Carp, in Scales bedrop'd with Gold,
Swift Trouts diversify'd with Crimson Stains,
And Pykes, the Tyrants of the watry plains.

Dr Johnson, the greatest of Augustan critics, said the poet should not number the streaks of the tulip; but that is just what Pope is doing here.

Thus, this greatest of Augustan poets transcended merely Augustan standards, was larger than his age: the writing of poetry was the only occupation for which this invalid was fit (and, indeed, had he been a stronger man, there was no honourable public employment open to a Papist). When he died in 1744, a year before the last Jacobite rebellion, he had, if we include his great versions of Homer, at 58 produced a more various, interesting, and copious volume of work than any English poet, except Shakespeare, to die at the same comparatively early age. The strange and complex personality which this great body of verse enables us to glimpse interests us more, today, perhaps, than it interested his comparatively psychologically incurious contemporaries. He is quite the oddest of our great poets.

These are reasons why Pope can be thought of as a poet for all time. But what has kept him from wide popularity is that he is very much of his own time, too; he prided himself on a subtle indirectness of allusion both to current gossip and to classical literary models, on a 'delicacy' with which, as we shall see, his blunt friend Swift reproached him. London, then as now, thought itself the centre of the world and gossiped excitedly, as it does now, about things and people unknown twenty miles outside its boundaries. Pope's 'delicacies' need a lot of elucidating; he puzzles us with trifles. That is why he has been recently a favourite subject of academic critics but still baffles (not because of his admirably clear style but because of his allusiveness) the ordinary sensitive reader who might get much from him. All that is original in this little study is that I try to help that ordinary reader by setting Pope in his age and relating his poems to the circumstances they were written in and the men or women they address or deal with. I try to set the reader in Pope's world; but the poetry for its own sake remains my central interest.

Pope died in what would today be counted early middle age (though, for a permanent invalid, in constant pain, he lived long) but his life spanned two completely different periods of English cultural history, the end of the Restoration and the beginning of the Augustan age. He was born after a century in which England, from the lucky Armada year of 1588 till the accession of William and Mary a few months after his birth, had been either threatened from abroad or torn by internal commotions. The reign of James I had been peaceful but inglorious. Then there had been the apparently auspicious beginning of Charles I's reign, followed by quarrels with Parliament, troubles with Ireland and Scotland, the Civil Wars, the King's execution, the Protectorate, the Restoration, the execution of some of the regicides, the inglorious Dutch wars, plots against the king, the Popish plot, Charles II's politically delayed death-bed declaration of his conversion to Rome, and the short reign of his blunt, stupid, honest brother James II, for many years an avowed Roman Catholic. In the hundred years before Pope's birth, neither the religious nor political system of Great Britain could be considered settled. We played a marginal and inept part in the general affairs of Europe. For painting we depended largely on foreign visitors, and our architecture, in spite of geniuses like Inigo Jones and Christopher Wren, would have been considered in the Rome of Bernini or the France of Versailles behind the times. Where Descartes was revolutionising the mind of Europe, Hobbes would be thought of as an English oddity ('coming to poetry, as he came to the mathematics, too late'). We prided ourselves on naturalness rather than decorum. Spite, jealousy, a readiness for merciless violence as in the Scottish Covenanters ('Jesus and no quarter!'), along with the mad eccentricity of sects like the Muggletonians, pervaded our religious life; on the orthodox side the fashionable arguments were like those of Marvell's enemy, Archdeacon Parker, Hobbesian and Erastian: it was our duty to adhere to the Church of England because it was the king's religion, not for any lights it carried in itself. In spite of a certain polish (and a certain libertinism both in sexual behaviour and, as typified by Lord Rochester's *Satyr against Mankind*, in religious thought) brought back by Charles II and his courtiers from their exile in France, a French visitor to England in 1688 would have found England a country backward in its arts and rustic in its manners. The savage hatred between the Whigs, a faction which united the great country magnates and the city merchants, and the Tories, which with equal incongruity united the staid minor country gentry and the gay courtiers, would have reminded such a Frenchman uncomfortably of the pointless but bloody skirmishes of Louis XIV's minority and Mazarin's ascendancy, the Fronde. The future of this weak and divided country would have seemed to the visitor a dark one.

In the year of Pope's death, 1744, the case was wholly altered. Though Roman Catholics like Pope still lay under some irksome disabilities, as did rich Protestant Nonconformists – which they got over by 'occasional conformity' or taking Anglican communion once a year, thus qualifying themselves for civic office – the old violent hatreds and prejudices had largely died away. One of Pope's closest friends was the saintly Anglican, Bishop Atterbury, for whom Pope spoke (inadequately and ineloquently) when the bishop was impeached for Jacobitism, later fleeing to exile in France; Pope's early fame secured him from his very early youth an entry into the greatest houses in England, the friendship of both Whig and Tory statesmen (whose differences, again, were by now much more about a competition for power than about passionately opposite principles). 'Mr Pope the Papist' might be an object of envious scorn for Grub Street pamphleteers, but not for his aristocratic friends; it is remarkable how easily this crippled youth, of humble stock who, from Spence's records of him, was an informative and obliging but not very witty or dominating conversationalist, took his place so early, as by right, among the men who ruled England. There must have been a special charm which neither his letters (carefully worked up by him for publication) nor Spence's records convey. The early portraits, in which one is struck by the large beautiful eyes, the graceful hands, and the sensitive mouth already beginning to be marked by habitual pain, may give us a hint of the sources of his magnetism. Invalid though he was, also, he was ready in his early years to assume among the young sprigs of the nobility the airs of an *insouciant* Restoration rake: to sit up late drinking and bantering though he knew that tomorrow he would be ill.

It could be said that in 1744 Pope's world – and the prestige of his own moralisings in poetry, of *An Essay on Man* and *Moral Essays (Epistles to Several Persons)*, contributed to this – was a more humane and civilised world than that into which he was born. It was, as has been emphasised already, his habit to emphasise the moral and social virtues and the central belief in a benevolent Deity which good men of all the Christian bodies, and even good men outside the Christian world, shared. *An Essay on Man,* published anonymously when he was already famous, was the most popular of all his poems and translated into an extraordinary variety of languages from Arabic to Welsh. It expressed exactly the kind of rational religiousness which dominated at least the first half of the eighteenth century. By 1744, there was no longer much libertinism or atheism of the Hobbesian sort (in France, even Voltaire, brought up by the Jesuits, for all his flippant or angry mockery of religious abuses believed to the last in a benevolent God and a moral universe). Newton had brought men back to the belief in a rational and benevolent deity; we did not, as Joseph Addison said in a famous hymn, actually *hear* the music of the spheres—there was no 'real music' there – but to look up at the sky was to be aware of the Divine Order.

By 1744, also, England was no longer a culturally or militarily weak country, a mere rustic province when one compared her with France. Newton, Locke, and to a lesser degree Berkeley (whose philosophy had much in common with that of the neo-Cartesian monk, Malebranche), enjoyed European fame. Voltaire's *Lettres sur les Anglais* and *Essai sur la Poésie épique* made the French aware of English liberty, of the self-respect and dignity of the rising merchant class, even of the genius of Milton (Shakespeare was a little more than Voltaire could take). As in Charles II's day English courtiers had larded their speech with French phrases, so Anglomania became the new folly of bright young people in France. England was also becoming, under the influence of the Palladianism of Pope's friend Lord Burlington and of landscape gardeners like Kent, a more elegant and picturesque country. Pope, whose hobby was painting (as a poet, especially in his sense of colour, he has a painter's eye), died before the rise of Reynolds and Gainsborough and the founder of English landscape painting, Richard Wilson. But Englishmen on the grand tour were buying with taste; the collection of Pope's enemy, Sir Robert Walpole, at Houghton was famous.

England had, after the War of the Spanish Succession, now taken France's place as the great military power in Europe.

Between 1688 and 1744 there had been other important changes, in the code of polite manners and in literary taste. The Restoration period (which we can take as lasting, for literary purposes, from Dryden's welcome to Charles II, *Astraea Redux*, in 1660 to his cynical *The Secular Masque* in the year of his death, 1700) has been, Professor James Sutherland has pointed out, the most aristocratic period in our literature. This does not mean that the Restoration is a period of great refinement and delicacy; it meant that 'the mob of gentlemen who wrote with ease' also wrote with dash but even more with scurrility, venom, and frank indecency. They were out to shock the Puritan citizens, whose wives, like Congreve's Mrs Fondlewife in *The Old Bachelor*, are regularly being seduced in Restoration comedies. They were disillusioned also with the romantic delicacy of feeling that had marked the wits of Charles I's court, Lovelace, Suckling, Carew (though it must be admitted that Aphra Behn and Rochester could write lyrics of great poignancy and delicacy and that Carew in his brilliantly and shockingly erotic *A Rapture* and *A Second Rapture* beats the Restoration erotic poets at their own game). They wrote lampoons, sometimes filthy, rather than true satire. It was the business, in the new century, of Addison and Steele to persuade their gentlemanly readers that it was possible to be witty and good company without being lewd; I am not sure that Pope, who always enjoyed a sly innuendo, ever wholly learned their lesson. He was to have some personal grudges against Addison, over his version of Homer, and from the first had noted that Addison's great conversational charm in his cups masked a priggish condescension. Certainly, the Tory wits, Swift, the Gay of *The Beggar's Opera* and Pope himself, retain to the last more than a touch of Restoration frankness. They moved in aristocratic circles, where perhaps the old broad jokes and openness and heartiness of manners still prevailed; Addison was more concerned with civilising the gentry, with introducing the new prosperous middle classes, like his Sir Andrew Freeport in the Coverly papers, to the enjoyment of literature.

Though Addison and Steele write pleasantly, few modern readers would turn to them, as they turn to Pope, Swift and Gay, for pleasure. Their importance is historical; they set themselves in the van of a new social tide. The seventeenth century had been an age of violent and quirky individualism. Addison and Steele mark the inauguration of an age of polite conformism; men now tended to sink their individuality in agreeableness and, apart from three or four writers of obstinate genius, including Pope, and one great philosopher with a touch of the visionary or the mystic in him, Berkeley, the first fifty years of the eighteenth century strike us as an insipid period. Locke, who with Newton dominated the thinking of the age, strikes us today as one of the clearest and most commonsensical but also one of the least exciting of English philosophers: he was also the most unpoetical: ''Tis a pleasant air,' he wrote of Parnassus, the Greek mountain which is the haunt of the Muses, 'but a barren soil'. Pope admired Newton, without understanding him, and indeed his great theodicy, or vindication of the ways of God to man, *An Essay on Man*, owes its power not to any originality of thought but to a mixture of lucidity and eloquence and to a harking back to the early Renaissance idea (also expressed in one of T. S. Eliot's favourite Elizabethan poems, Sir John Davies's *Orchestra*) of the great chain of being. Pope saw Marlborough, the great captain who had made Great Britain, so weak when Pope was born, the greatest nation in Europe, as his friends of the Tory party, St John and Harley saw him, as an avaricious man prolonging the War of the Spanish Succession for his own profit and hanging on to power at home through the power of his Duchess, the beautiful virago Sarah, with Queen Anne. Except perhaps at the time of the Treaty of Utrecht, when Pope was at one with all good men in the nation in welcoming peace and prosperity at the end of *Windsor Forest*, with its invocation of the Thames as the great new channel of commerce, Pope was always a little out of tune with the currents of his age. Walpole was the minister of peace and prosperity, an infinitely greater statesman than Pope's dead friend Oxford and his living friend Bolingbroke, but Walpole's coarseness disgusted as did the boorishness of King George II, who hated 'bainters and boets'. Pope's personal religion is best described as a kind of Christianising deism, or a Christianity so ecumenical that its chief emphasis was on the belief in a powerful, beneficent deity of inscrutable purposes and the virtue it praised most was the social bene-volence that God has arranged to grow naturally out of our innate self-love. His loyalty to the Roman Catholic religion also turned the Grub Street scribblers against him; though it was not, as the above description shows, a loyalty of either a bigoted or irrational kind. It was partly something he owed to his parents; partly it sprang from a genuine admiration for the Christian humanism (rejected by Luther and Calvin as it was largely rejected by the Church of Rome) of Erasmus.

Yet nothing could be more mistaken than to suppose that Pope, because he took the unpopular side, lived in a state of social neglect and isolation. Addison was the typical man of the age, and Addison had his worldly rewards: an unhappy marriage to a Countess, to whose rakish son, Pope's friend, Lord Warwick, he had been tutor; and a post as Secretary of State in which his preoccupation with the style rather than the matter of the state papers he prepared rendered him practically useless. But Addison was happiest and most at ease in the company of men of his own type, the literary journalist ex-don. As a Papist, Pope had had none of Addison's advantages; he had two short experiences, and unfortunate ones, in seminaries run for Catholics followed by private education at home, where Pope's father encouraged his son's 'rhymes'. Even if Pope's poor and steadily declining health had made such projects feasible, admission to either of the two great universities was as firmly forbidden to a Roman Catholic as any kind of public office.

Yet Pope, in the most straightforward of snobbish senses, seems always to have lived in better company than Addison. 'Granville the polite', who encouraged Pope's earliest verses, was a nobleman, statesman, and minor poet of the distinguished family connection that had earlier brought forth Sir Richard Grenville of the *Revenge*, and Sir Bevil Granvil, who held the West Country in support of King Charles I. The 'delicacy' on which Pope prided himself as a poet would include a delicate appreciation of such histories and connections. Another early friend was the ageing playwright Wycherley, whom Pope met in his youth and helped with his inept late verses, and who, he remembered afterwards, 'had the true nobleman look'. Harley, Earl of Oxford and Earl Mortimer, and his Secretary of State, Henry St John, Viscount Bolingbroke, were at daggers drawn with each other in Queen Anne's last year – Harley felt it would be equally fatal and divisive to the Tory party to declare either for James III, the Old Pretender, or George, Elector of Hanover, the Protestant successor; Bolingbroke would have risked the Pretender – but they were united in their love and admiration for Pope.

They lost office shortly before Anne's death, Harley's drunkenness (he drank heavily because his political problem about the succession was in theory and practice insoluble) resulting in the handing over of his wand of office to the Duke of Shrewsbury. On the arrival of George I, Harley was temporarily imprisoned in the tower and St John fled to France to bore himself to death at the Pretender's pious miniature court at St Germain. But politics was no longer the bloody and bigoted business it had been when Pope was born. Oxford was soon released to retire to his estates and to his beloved books; St John was allowed to sneak peacefully home, became a leading spokesman of opposition to Walpole and the leader of young sprigs of the anti-Walpole faction, but was never to enjoy power again (or even permission to sit and speak in the House of Lords) and became something of a nuisance even to his own supporters. It is not unjust to what we know of Bolingbroke's character to suggest that he would not have busied himself so much with Pope's poetry (*An Essay on Man* owed much to Bolingbroke's advice and there are those who say that

9

Bolingbroke injected deistic arguments knowing the unphilosophical poet would not perceive them) if he had had more solid and profitable employments to his hand.

The men of letters who were Pope's closest friends, Swift, Gay, Arbuthnot (one a great, the next a good, and the third, if we allow for the local nature of his political satire, an interesting writer) all moved in similar circles. In his youth, Sir William Trumbull, a former Secretary of State to William III, took an interest in the boy's precocious genius and took him on health-giving rides around Windsor Forest. The Catholic gentry patronised him, including Martha ('Patty') and Theresa Blount, of whom the first was to become his closest woman friend and, Mr F. W. Bateson thinks, his mistress. Certainly his friendship with Martha lasted a lifetime, unlike his adoration for Lady Mary Wortley Montagu (to whom, on her departure to Turkey with her husband, the new Ambassador to the Sublime Porte, Pope's *Eloisa to Abelard* is a kind of love poem), which changed, through causes that are still a mystery, to a most bitter and scurrilous hatred. Such quarrels with some friends and such falls from powers of others did not prevent Pope from moving among what were then called 'the great' to the end of his life. He was welcome at the opposition court of George II's son Frederick, Prince of Wales, with its young political advisers Chester. field and Pulteney. He was equally friends with the most charming woman in England, Henrietta Hobart, Mrs Howard, Countess of Suffolk, the official mistress of George II. (They lounged away a boring hour together each evening, as George felt that he owed it to his position to have an official mistress; Henrietta was aware that he was too boorish, stupid, and self-conceited to appreciate her wit and that his only real physical passion was for his wife, the shrewd, practical, and learned Queen Caroline, who ruled him with her mind and was emotionally his slave.)

For all his humble origins, Pope demanded of his friends either genius or breeding. The only ill-bred and stupidly self-conceited man of whom he ever made a friend was Warburton, later a bishop, and famous, if at all, for Dr Johnson's sardonic comments on his edition of Shakespeare, and an absurdly sophistical work of theology, *The Divine Legation of Moses*, which proves the genuineness of Moses's mission by the fact that he never, as any impostor would have, promised the Jews the gift of eternal life after death. Warburton was a bully and may have bullied the ageing Pope; his posthumous edition of Pope re-arranges poems and changes titles in an unforgivable way. He loathed Martha

Blount. But Pope took him up on account of the one disinterested act in Warburton's loathsome life: Warburton, before he knew Pope or could expect any benefit from him, while, indeed, the poem was still published anonymously, defended *An Essay on Man* against the Swiss Professor Crousaz's accusations of deliberate heresy. It was a tepid defence: doubtful passages were merely declared capable of an orthodox interpretation. But Pope, whose feelings both of friendship and anger were always warm, was permanently grateful.

Yet Warburton, among Pope's friends, was an exception and an unfortunate one. Proud and independent though he was, Pope was not typical of an age that saw in Defoe the beginnings of that typically middle-class form, the novel, and in Addison and Steele the preaching of an upper-middle-class morality. He was most at home in these aristocratic circles in which something of the Restoration and its freedom of sexual innuendo survived, as it does in Belinda's lament at the end of Canto IV of the revised version of *The Rape of the Lock*:

> Oh hadst thou, Cruel! been content to seize
> Hairs less in sight, or any Hairs but these!

That was a young man's poem, but the bawdily funny *Sober Advice from Horace* (with its very funny scholarly notes, mocking the irascible style of the great Greek and Latin textual critic, Dr Bentley) was the work of a middle-aged moralist; and it was published with the thinnest veil of anonymity. In his letters, even to ladies, Pope could be very outspoken. Increasingly an invalid though he was throughout his life, there is no reason to think that the two early accidents which cost him height, strength, and health (being trampled by a cow near his father's warehouse in London and by a queer coincidence acquiring Potts's disease, or a tendency towards curvature and weakening of the spine, by drinking the diseased milk of another cow when his father had retired to the country), destroyed his normal sexual feelings, no doubt as intense as all his other feelings. Perhaps the imagination dwells on what the body can rarely or never hope to accomplish. It is worth noting that among Pope's juvenilia are imitations of the Caroline and Restoration 'mob of gentlemen who wrote with ease' and who wrote, from time to time, very freely. Though Pope accepts on the surface all the new Augustan canons of correctness and decorum, something of the Restoration *diable au corps*, vivacity, impudence, and desire to shock, still remains with him. One of the few authors outside his own circle for whom his admiration was whole-hearted was Congreve, the last great survivor of the Restoration spirit; and his earliest literary friend of reputation and collaborator (grown alas senile and sometimes tetchy, though courteous at heart) was the founding father of Restoration comedy, 'manly' Wycherley. Even his friend Gay's *The Beggar's Opera*, though quite unlike Restoration comedy and in a sense one of the wholly 'original' works in English literature, is very free-spoken and very unlike the mawkish sentimental comedy of Steele. Pope, the greatest writer and the presiding spirit of our Augustan age, is himself Augustan only if we use the word with a tactful latitude.

We can also paradoxically assert that though Pope is our greatest verse satirist, his natural genius is *not* for satire. Satire aims at the type, not the individual, the vice or folly not the man: if the cap fits wear it; if a satirist points out some faults of ours, we should silently correct them, and be grateful. Thus Dryden's portrait of Zimri in *Absalom and Achitophel* was based on the second and last Duke of Buckingham (there was to be a Duke of Buckingham, whom Pope knew, but not of the brilliant Villiers family), but it is a masterpiece because it represents a permanently recurring type, the man of charm, talent, and energy who comes to nothing because he cannot stick at one thing, has no sea-mark or steering-point. Buckingham recognised the essential truth of the portrait and was not in the least resentful.

But Pope's Sporus in the *Epistle to Dr Arbuthnot* is not a portrait of a recurrent type. It is the actual Lord Hervey of George II's Court or it is the Devil or a Chimera, neither of them (the utterly evil or the non-existent) suitable subjects for satire. A reader of Hervey's memoirs – a masterpiece in their way, an English miniature equivalent for the great memorialist of the court of Louis XIV and the Regency, the Duc de St-Simon – will recognise that, unpleasant though Hervey was in a number of ways, this scream of rage does not evoke the real Hervey. The real Hervey was capable of love, courage, and loyalty especially towards his patron, Queen Caroline. He was emotionally attracted towards his own sex, but normal enough to marry the beauty of the Court, Molly Lepell, and have eight children by her, and also to seduce the Prince of Wales's mistress, Miss Wade. Permanent invalid though he was (and it was unforgivable for Pope, himself a permanent invalid, to sneer at Hervey for his special diet, calling him a 'mere white Curd of asses' milk'), he was brave enough to risk his life in a duel, forced on him by an insult, with the sturdy Pulteney. Far from being the lick-spittle whom Pope depicts, Hervey, after years of loyal service as Walpole's intermediary with Queen Caroline, who was herself

Walpole's intermediary with the King, told 'the great man' (Walpole's general nickname) that he understood politics and expected neither gratitude nor reward for his service. Pope's great portrait of Sporus is memorable not in an Augustan way – Dr Johnson thought it a 'mean' piece of writing – but rather in the way that many Romantic poems are memorable, as a kind of release, for Pope, of dark and painful emotions. The satires give us Pope's emotions about people (glorified pictures of Harley and St John, an often unfair spite against those whom he mildly dislikes, an almost hysterical savagery against those whom he considers real enemies) rather than people in themselves. The satires, in fact, are personal to the last degree, and their value, in the end, is that of a vivid and various self-portrait: whomever else he misrepresents, Pope never misrepresents himself. He gives us, in a word, a man and his world, and fascinating though the world is, it is, as with all great poets, the man who is finally at the centre of our interest.

2
Pope's Character and History

Pope found his personal history very interesting and even arranged in later life for the surreptitious publication of volumes of his letters; this would excuse him publishing 'corrected' – in fact, often elaborately rewritten – versions without the appearance of egotism. In fact the personal charm which, at least as a young man up to the publication of his first collected volume of 1717, he undoubtedly possessed is not vividly conveyed either in his own letters, even when these are not touched up, or in any contemporary account of him. There are hints of its nature in his early portraits; but the wittiest of English poets has left no striking examples of conversational wit. As to his moral character, biographers have until recently tended to put too much emphasis on his poetic and personal vanity, the personal spite that demonstrates itself sometimes in his satire, some examples of unkind jokes apparently at the expense of benefactors or friends (like the portrait of Mrs Howard in the moral epistle on the character of women or the possible spite against a great nobleman who had done Pope no harm in the description of Timon's villa in the same group of epistles) and too little on Pope's virtues. Pope often refers to these virtues, to his devotion to his parents or to his contemptuous generosity towards his Grub Street enemies, to his role as the general defender of virtue in a corrupt age:

> Yes, I am proud. I must be proud to see
> Men not afraid of God, afraid of me,

and all these attitudes are today strange to our emotional and social habits. We are much more aware than Pope was of the importance of forbearance; we feel that, if we have any virtues, it is for others not ourselves to point them out; and that some virtues, in any case, like devotion to an ageing parent, should be taken for granted. Our notions of psychology are again much more complex than those of Pope –

though very few of us could equal him in actual acuteness of observation of human behaviour – and his notion that every man is governed by a 'ruling passion' (and every woman partly by volatility and partly the fact that 'ev'ry Woman is at heart a Rake') strikes us as absurdly over-simple. Clear and straightforward as Pope's verse is, a model of concise clarity, its wealth of topical allusions asks for hard work from the reader; and its moral attitudes, though we would find it hard to say why, seem odder to us, in his complimentary verse as much as in his satire, than those of any other English poet of equal greatness.

Pope, as we have seen, was born early in 1788, the son of the second marriage of a prosperous linen-draper who was also a Catholic convert. Old Mr Pope lived over his warehouse in Lombard Street but, when James II fled and William and Mary succeeded, it became the law that Roman Catholics must live at least fifteen miles away from the Cities of London and Westminster. William, however, was no tyrant and it was not till 1700 that the elder Alexander Pope finally settled in a small farm, Binfield, in Windsor Forest, taking his savings with him. He kept his money in large wooden boxes – perhaps he distrusted William's new Bank of England – and helped himself to it as he needed it. As we have seen, probably at Lombard Street (where a milkmaid with a cow travelled round the city, milking her animal at customers' doors) but possibly in Binfield Pope had been trampled on by a large cow. Later, from drinking bad milk from one of the Binfield cows, he developed that disease of curvature of the spine which made it necessary, in his later years, for him to be sewn every morning into a tight pair of corsets and to have his withered legs warmed and disguised by three thick pairs of woollen stockings. He was almost a dwarf, well under five feet high (four feet six, in fact). What is particularly sad is that his earliest portrait, painted before these accidents, shows a chubby, cheerful little boy with every promise of healthy growth. Though these accidents had been very far from destroying sexual desire in Pope, to women, even at their kindest, Pope must have seemed a doll or a toy (if Martha Blount, as Mr Bateson thinks, became his mistress, affection and sympathy, perhaps pity, rather than the passion of lust must have been her motives). It was notable throughout his life, however, that women – perhaps because they did not consider him seriously as a sexual object – were ready to make friends of him and confide in him.

Pope had been to two schools for Catholics in London, learning little or nothing. At Binfield his father set him to writing 'rhymes' and some of his early efforts survive, mainly neat imitations of the earlier court poets of his own century, though there is also a bawdy imitation of Chaucer. He was busy also with translations from Latin and even Greek (the famous heroic Sarpedon episode from the *Iliad*). He was never in any profound sense a scholar. Self-taught, like many poetic translators, he learned the syntax of his original from the sense rather than the sense from the syntax. He was shameless, as in his great version of Homer written between his thirtieth and fortieth years, in consulting earlier English and also French versions of the texts he worked on, partly as cribs, partly to study the taste and diction of various periods of modern verse. He had also ambitions towards original verse. A projected epic came to nothing, but he had roughed out and shown to friends his first pastorals before 1705, the year in which he renewed his acquaintance with Wycherley. His attempts to turn into smooth verse the last products of Wycherley's wandering mind led to tetchiness, but the big irascible dying old bear and the tiny genius from the country retained a lasting affection for each other. Earlier still, at the age of twelve, in the last year of Dryden's life, the young Pope had been taken to see a greater writer enthroned at Wills's coffee house; he gazed on Dryden with awe but was acute enough to see that Dryden belonged to the world of books and writers not, as Pope himself was to belong, to the world of polished society.

Something has been said in the first chapter about the surprising range of Pope's social circle even as an unpublished poet in his teens. At first, this seems surprising. Old Mr Pope was not himself a man of any particular social pretensions or distinctions, but Windsor Forest was a favourite haunt of Catholic recusant families, like the Blounts, and Catholics clung together with a certain disregard for fine, or even broad, social distinctions that might not have been found among Protestants. We should also remember the enormous importance attached by well-bred and educated people, in Pope's age, to poetic talent. No other age could, perhaps, have produced a didactic poem with the line:

Nature's chief Masterpiece is writing well.

Until Burlington took up architecture, poetry (in which drama was included) was the only art in which a gentleman could seriously interest himself. Vanbrugh was far more famous for his comedies than for Blenheim; Wren owed his knighthood to his strenuous career as a public servant rather than to any public sense of the glory of St Paul's. Hawksmoor, the most original architect of his age, got his commissions, but lived and died obscurely. Pope's hobby was painting, but when he mentions Sir Godfrey Kneller it is as a joke. There was a feeling that England was, up to the time when Burlington revived Palladio and Kent and 'Capability' Brown created the idea of the informal garden, rustic and backward in the visual arts. Even when this sense of backwardness had vanished, the status of the painter and the architect, working for money for clients, was uncertain: Sir Joshua Reynolds, President of the Royal Academy, is certainly a gentleman in Boswell but Boswell has nothing to say about two greater and more important painters, Hogarth and Gainsborough. But throughout the century a poet of real talent (and Johnson and Crabbe were humbler in origin than Pope) counted, as soon as his gifts were recognised, as the social equal of the greatest. Poetry was never more generally honoured than in what Matthew Arnold thought the most unpoetical of centuries. Pope had another advantage. He had no rivals. If we think of the century before Pope, there are Milton and Dryden, and before them Shakespeare and Jonson. Between 1709, when he began to publish, and 1744, when he died, there were minor poets of talent, but no one who could even begin to compete with Pope. Even his more intelligent enemies must have recognised him as a great English asset; unrivalled, for instance, in France.

But, apart from the special prestige of the poet in Pope's time, he must have had even in boyhood an elusive charm. Old Sir William Trumbull, who had been William III's Secretary of State, lured the lad away from his books for healthy rides through Windsor Forest. The pretty and well-bred Blount girls were not offended with little Pope's sometimes broad gallantries. Garth, the author of a burlesque poem called *The Dispensary* (which, together with Boileau's *Le Lutrin*, may have given Pope some hints for the more elegant mock-heroic manner of *The Rape of the Lock*) encouraged the young poet, as did Walsh whom Dryden had described as the best critic in England. It was Walsh who told Pope that we had had great English poets before but never one who was correct and it was correctness, above all, that Pope should aim at. What *exactly* Walsh meant it is hard to know: Pope is in fact a brilliant but uneven writer and, far from aiming at a slow laborious correctness, he said that he wrote best when he wrote most rapidly. He was now also making London acquaintances. It was probably Trumbull who introduced him to Wycherley; Wycherley, unfortunately, introduced him to John Dennis.

Purely literary society, if it lacked an aristocratic flavour, was never much to Pope's taste. He was ill at ease in Addison's circle of subservient mediocrities; Pope, younger, less outwardly impressive, loathed mediocrities and knew that he was, unlike the talented Addison, a genius. Though he had no political ambitions or strictly political passions, during the short period before Queen Anne's death when the Tories, under Harley and St John were in power, he had been very near the centre of things, and he liked being at the centre. All his life, it pleased him that great lords and ladies should seek out his company merely because he was a great poet; the *Epistle to Dr Arbuthnot* makes it clear that the homage and the requests for help of inferior poets wearied him and did not even flatter his vanity. He doubted their sincerity and distrusted their judgment. It is not surprising, as the preface to *The Dunciad* shows, that Pope was not merely the most famous poet of his age but the one most bitterly loathed by inferior writers.

Between 1709, with the publication of the *Pastorals*, and 1714, with the publication of the revised version of his early masterpiece, *The Rape of the Lock*, Pope's reputation as a poet steadily grew. When he published his collected early works in his twenty-ninth year in 1717, he stood alone. In 1716, Pope's father sold the house at Binfield and he moved to Chiswick, to be nearer his new friend Lord Burlington, who taught him his taste for Palladian architecture, and whose little Roman villa, a learned man's toy, at Chiswick can still be admired. Pope had, in spite of his intimacy with the Tories, now fallen from power with the Hanoverian succession, indulging in a largely imaginary passion for the great Whig beauty, Lady Mary Wortley Montagu. She was a woman of strong 'masculine' common sense (famous for introducing to England the Turkish practice of inoculation against small pox by injections of cow pox) and coarse and hearty sexual appetites. He expresses a high-flown devotion to her at the end of one of the two new poems in the 1717 volume, *Eloisa to Abelard*. Then, on her return to England, Lady Mary managed to hurt his vanity, and his subsequent references to her are venomous and obscene. His true and life-long friend among women (Theresa rather dropped from the scene) was Martha or 'Patty' Blount. She was not brilliant; by middle age she had lost much of the grace of bearing, bloom of complexion, and perhaps even sweetness of expression that had at first attracted him. But she cared for him with the tenderness of a nurse, and it was understood that when the great Mr Pope was invited for a weekend visit the commonplace Miss Blount must come too. Even Warburton, who loathed her, admitted that when Pope was on his last sick-bed her entrance would stir him into new cheerfulness and life (Frieda Lawrence and Maria Huxley both had the same gift for reviving the sick D. H. Lawrence).

1717 was the triumphant year of Pope's life, but saddened by the death of his father. In 1718, he moved with his mother to a new house at Twickenham, which was to be his last place of permanent residence. He amused himself there with constructing a grotto, a kind of gnomes' cave full of glittering crystals. But his happy early life was at an end. From 1715, Homer was his chief labour over ten years (if we make allowance for two striking original poems, *Elegy to the Memory of an Unfortunate Lady* and *Eloisa to Abelard* at the end of the 1717 volume and a very beautiful dedication of Thomas Parnell's poems, which he had posthumously edited, to Harley after Harley's release from the Tower) and the long daily labours of translation had a permanent effect on Pope's temper and health. In 1717, he had still a youthful gaiety; by 1726 years of comparative solitude and long daily hours of labour stooped over his table had made him a man older than his years. It was now that Pope's formidable powers of verse invective suddenly appeared, as well, fortunately, as a gift for lighter and gayer conversational satire, busied with minor follies, in a Horatian tone.

Pope had been attacked by many envious fools and had ignored the attacks. His fury in his first great satire, *The Dunciad*, was aroused by Theobald's on the whole well-merited strictures on Pope's edition of Shakespeare, a task for which Pope was unequipped either by any gift for textual emendation or any wide reading in Elizabethan and Jacobean drama. *The Dunciad*, of which the first version came out in 1728, is a mock-epic like *The Rape of the Lock*, but as dark and thunderous as the other poem is sparkling and light. Pope was used enough to being attacked for being a cripple, a Papist, a Jacobite (untrue), a monster of self-conceit. The attacks dated back to John Dennis's thunderous reply to a few carefully wounding lines in *An Essay on Criticism* of 1711, but never seemed to move him. (Probably the coarse attacks on his physical deformity did. There is a story of his saying: 'These things are my diversion!' his face contorted with agony.) Whatever his feelings, Pope had the sense, up to 1728, to know that silence shows contempt.

I think Theobald's attack started him off on his war on Grub Street for a paradoxical reason: Theobald's attack is largely just. Theobald was a small writer but, in a later period of Shakespeare studies, he might have been a very considerable textual scholar. His emendation in *Henry V* of the Hostess's 'and a Table of greenefields' to 'and 'a babled of green fields' is still almost universally accepted. (There is a modern theory that Shakespeare's text can be justified if one understands the allusion as topical, to Sir Richard Grenville of the *Revenge*: 'and a Table of Greenfields', meaning 'and a very picture of Grenville's', who had also a nose as sharp as a pen. If this conjecture is right one has still an uneasy feeling that Theobald has improved on Shakespeare.)

Men of genius find just criticism the hardest to bear. Pope knew very little Greek, and could not have translated Homer without the aid of earlier translations, English, French, and Latin; his coolness with Addison dates from Addison's encouragement of Tickell's rival version of Homer: Pope knew he could beat Tickell any day as a poet but was much his inferior as a scholar. Similarly Pope never forgave Dr Bentley, one of the very great textual critics of Greek and Latin literature of all time, for 'It is a pretty poem, Mr Pope, but you must not call it *Homer*'. His dislike of the Royal Society (apart from the conventional homage which must be paid to Newton) and of studies in our older poetry which he had not shared ('And beastly Skelton Heads of Houses quote') show a fundamental intellectual error in *The Dunciad*: what Pope thinks pedantry is often true scholarship. At another level, the moral one, is it right or necessary to attack bad writing as such (it will surely perish of its own badness, quietly) and to mock Grub Street scribblers for their poverty (it is true they could earn a better living by taking up some quietly useful trade, but one cannot help remembering, when Pope rubs in their poverty, that, though scrupulously charitable with his income, he was a rich man compared to them). *The Dunciad*, and particularly the Fourth Book of Pope's late revision of the poem, with Colley Cibber instead of Theobald as the new hero, is Pope's most powerful sustained piece of original writing. It is also unpleasant in its general mood and in many places positively nasty. Pope's excuse might have been that he was warning England against a complete decay of culture, a reign of Dullness: the rest of the century shows that such fears were fantasies.

But Pope could have made a plausible moral defence of himself. *The Dunciad* suddenly showed the hack writers who had sneered at Pope with impunity for years that they were more vulnerable than he was; mercilessly, he exposed their servility and inconsistency, their veerings between flattery and insolence, their low creeping talents, their failure, their poverty. These last attacks, from his own stance of elegance and comfort (though it was also a stance of perpetual physical pain and perpetual shame at his own deformity) I have admitted to finding the least forgivable aspects of the poem. But the illusion of literary talent is still the most widespread of illusions. Pope felt, as when he wrote in the *Epistle to Dr Arbuthnot* about the clerk,

> Who pens a Stanza when he should *engross*,

that nobody is compelled to write. Pope did not see himself as mocking poverty: he saw himself as defending these literary standards, typified by himself, Swift, Gay, and Arbuthnot, that had reached their height in the last years of Queen Anne under the benign rule of Harley and St John. He is writing in *The Dunciad* not light Horatian but Juvenalian tragical satire, which at moments (particularly in the final pages of the fourth book added almost at the end of his life) is not a mockery of the sublime but the true sublime. The end of the fourth book of the revised *Dunciad* has a Miltonic grandeur.

The end of the long and often tedious labour of Homer and the relief of getting rid of his spleen in *The Dunciad* now released in Pope an extraordinary burst of energy. He had long had two great ambitions. One was to write a great philosophical poem, at once vindicating the ways of God to man and helping man to understand, and to accept with humility, his own high but subordinate rank in the scheme of creation. Pope intended to supplement *An Essay on Man* with a considerable number of moral essays, of which he completed four under the title of *Epistles to Several Persons*. On his death-bed, Warburton persuaded him to change the title to *Moral Essays*. The epistles were intended to illustrate in a more vivid and concrete way the rather generalised ethical theorising of *An Essay on Man*. The scheme of the *Moral Essays* allowed for a humour and vivacity (much more light-hearted than the savage spleen of *The Dunciad*) which displays Pope's natural wit and charm but which would have been out of place among the solemnities of *An Essay on Man*.

It is doubtful if *An Essay on Man*, the most widely admired of Pope's poems in his own day, still ranks as a great philosophical poem. The most acute of the critics nearly contemporary with Pope, Dr Johnson, a very devout and very troubled Christian, found its optimism obvious and shallow. Its scheme owed a great deal to prose hints from Bolingbroke, who was a deist, but not everything. There is no reason to suppose that Pope, with his recurrent insistence on the importance of charity, was not influenced, as he himself insisted, by Pascal's *Pensées* and by the *Télémaque* which Fénelon, the tutor of Louis XIV's grand-son, the Duc de Bourgogne, had written to instruct and reform his illustrious pupil. Reformation was needed. The Duc de Bourgogne was a brilliant but ferocious young man, who in his fits of rage smashed up furniture, who for his amusement blew up frogs with gunpowder, and who combined an inordinate lust for women very unusually, as Saint Simon discreetly puts it, 'with a passion of a quite different sort'. Fénelon turned Bourgogne into something like a saint; too much of a saint, Saint-Simon feared, for all his own narrow and intense piety, for a future king. Fénelon had effected this reformation by putting all his stress on the second great commandment: 'Love thy neighbour as thyself.' In describing how God has given us self-love so that it may blossom out into social love, Pope, a true Christian humanist, is speaking in the spirit, though not in the language of Fénelon and the Gospels.

Yet, after all these labours on the heights, Pope was, as we can already observe in the *Epistles to Several Persons*, feeling a need to relax and be more natural; the need for a quicker, lighter, more personal, more volatile tone. He found his model in the satires and epistles of Horace. His *Imitations of Horace*, published with the Latin *en face*, gave Pope a chance, transferring Horace to the London of George II, to be his own natural self, almost over-generous to his friends (his admira-tion for Bolingbroke, whose whole life was a flashily acted part, was absurd, yet one admires Pope's capacity for hero-worship more than one reproves his credulity); always warm where he speaks with moral approval or gratitude; bitterly and excessively sharp to his foes when he thinks them, like Lord Hervey and Lady Mary, malignant; blandly severe, but balanced and just, to a dead man like Addison, who was not a true friend or an open enemy, but whose gifts as well as his faults deserved recognition. After the sustained narrative of Homer and the attempt at sustained argument of *An Essay on Man*, Pope can now be quirky, short-winded, a weather-cock, himself; now fierce, now tender; now in despair for his country under the coarse, mercenary rule of Walpole and the boorish German sovereignty of George II, with the rough vulgarian Colley Cibber dominating what had been the stage of Congreve, Vanbrugh, and Gay; now overcome with wild laughter at the farce of life. If Pope's central gift in poetry was (as I believe it may have been) variety of tone, rapid modulation of mood, the *Imitations of Horace*, for those who like myself love the man as well as the poet, are his most centrally revealing work.

These poems are, in fact, a self-portrait. The surreptitious publication of a selection of his letters by his useful butt and tool, the bookseller (which then also implied a publisher) Curll, gave Pope the chance to enlarge the self-portrait in prose by his own carefully reworked edition of his letters published with his official approval in 1737. They are likely to appear to most modern readers, as to my friend Martin Seymour Smith, affected and insincere, with an eye on the possible public reader rather than the correspondent. But they *are* reworked, and even occasionally assigned to correspondents other than their actual recipients, and such untouched letters as survive are more natural; yet it must be admitted that, even in letters where he was not thinking of ultimate publication, Pope, even in his youth, wrote to impress. Pope fortunately arranged that his correspondence with Swift, the only writer of equal genius he had known, and one of the few men with whom he could be utterly at ease, should be published separately. They remained the closest of friends, but Swift's last visit to Pope on his last trip from Ireland, when he was stricken with deafness and melancholy and Pope was a suffering invalid, was a sad occasion, bringing little gaiety to either man, though spoilt by no quarrel. Between 1727 and 1732, four volumes of miscellanies in prose and verse written by Pope, Swift, and other members of the Martinus Scriblerus club were published. They reflect the grim motto of Swift's later life when, exiled in Dublin, he sought the most trivial diversions: '*Vive la bagatelle!*' The idea of Martinus Scriblerus was one of those conceptions that are more amusing in thought than in execution. *The Memoirs of Martinus Scriblerus* was a satire on pedantry, better done by Swift earlier in *The Tale of a Tub* and *The Battle of the Books* and later in the Academy of Lagado (a skit on the Royal Academy) in the third book of *Gulliver's Travels*. Pope's own prose, apart from his prefaces and notes to his Homer, is on the whole disappointing. What is still worth reading in *Martinus Scriblerus* is the *Peri Bathous, or the Art of Sinking in Poetry*, with its many awful examples of false and inflated writing from Pope's and Swift's contemporaries.

In 1737, Pope – the great burst of late energy seemed to be subsiding – published two more Horatian imitations, but was deeply distressed by an attack on *An Essay on Man* by a Swiss Calvinist clergyman, Crousaz, Professor of Mathematics at the University of Lausanne. Crousaz felt that Pope's argument, though no doubt Pope did not realise this, led to a deterministic pantheism like Spinoza's: for whom God and Nature are the same, for whom 'everything is perfect of its

C

kind', and for whom our 'intellectual love of God' is a love that can ask no return. Pope, of course, was incapable of such sublime and original ideas as those of the great Dutch-Jewish philosopher. Warburton, as has been noted, replied to Crousaz, not claiming that Pope's position was necessarily totally valid but that the arguments from plenitude (God must work out all the logical possibilities of His decision to create a world) and from the great chain of being were traditionally accepted as orthodox. Pope was delighted to meet Warburton in 1740 and relied heavily on the lumpish, greedy and ambitious, ungraciously self-important pedant's advice possibly in the more metaphysical passages, very obscure ones, of the fourth book of *The Dunciad* and certainly in planning a complete posthumous edition of his works in his last years.

In his original *Dunciad* and in his imitations of Horace, Pope had taken occasional flings at Colley Cibber. But for Pope, Cibber, a professional actor turned indifferent playwright (and never in the first rank even as an actor), would be remembered only as Lord Foppington in *The Relapse* and as the author of memoirs which are a very useful contribution to his history of the theatre. A cheerful extrovert, Cibber lacked vanity, and it is to himself that we owe Congreve's comment on his first comedy: 'There is something here which is very like wit, but it is not wit.' The near-wit, however, was amusing enough to audiences to keep Cibber prosperously busy for many years on the stage. He was under no illusion that he was making a permanent contribution to literature. But in 1742, after reading *The New Dunciad*, the first version of Book IV, in which Theobald is still the hero, but Cibber is described as lying comfortably on the lap of Dulness, this pert, complacent, but fundamentally not ill-natured little man was mildly stirred. Why did Mr Pope choose to make so free with his name? (Maynard Mack thinks that Pope was using Cibber as a kind of substitute for George II and Walpole whose grossness it would not have been prudent to attack quite so directly.)

In July 1742, Cibber published *A Letter from Mr Cibber to Mr Pope*. No doubt, he admitted, Pope was a much better writer, but did that matter so much? Cibber had earned his bread honestly and, if Pope found his writing mean or ridiculous, he had merely to refrain from reading Cibber. But there was a line of Pope's about Cibber still having his 'Lord and Whore', and perhaps Pope was perpetually remembering a favour Cibber had once done Pope. Years ago, when Pope played the role of a gay young man about town, Cibber and

Pope had gone to a brothel together and, realising that the poet might catch a disease there that would ultimately destroy his wits, Cibber had snatched away 'this little hasty Hero, like a terrible *Tom Tit*, pertly perching upon the Mount of Love'. The episode, in phrasing and conception, is at least a brilliant exercise of the comic imagination (Cibber had humour, whether or not he had wit). What was worse, it might have actually happened, and Pope certainly could not prove it had not. There is an early poem in quatrains in which Pope describes himself as the 'gayest Valetudinaire. Most thinking Rake alive' and says that now he is leaving London his noble and wild young friends must 'knock up Whores alone'. The maddening thing was that Pope had quite unnecessarily provoked Cibber, who was not a malignant man. In his lively and good-natured *Apology for the Life of Mr Colley Cibber* Cibber (as well as quoting, without resentment, Congreve's just criticism of him) had merely mildly complained that Pope was 'a little free' with him.

The result of Pope's rage was that he published in 1743 a totally revised four-book version of *The Dunciad* with Cibber replacing Theobald as the hero. There was unfortunately no resemblance between Theobald, a scholar of retiring habits whose criticism of Pope's Shakespeare had been based on a thorough study of what to the Augustans was the obscure, archaic drama of the Elizabethan and Jacobean ages and the cheerful, social Cibber who, except to steal a plot from Molière, hardly ever looked at a book. But Pope was not so much dealing with persons as creating a kind of myth of the triumph of Dulness; in this kind of epic, or mock-epic, it was essential to the idea of the hero that he should attempt nothing of worth and achieve nothing at all, and be in the end a mere lay figure. From that point of view, Cibber suited Pope as well as Theobald, they were both figures in a dark myth. To some contemporary critics the myth was too dark. Dr Johnson loathed the excremental images which mark the fourth book of *Gulliver's Travels* as they mark especially the second book of *The Dunciad* and thought that Swift's foulness of mind had, on one of his last visits to England, corrupted Pope's comparative innocence. Certainly there are no touches of nastiness in the *Works* of 1717.

We should make allowance, perhaps, for the fact that scatological humour was a literary tradition: Rabelais was grosser than either Swift or Pope, but because of his obviously gay, ebullient temperament nobody has been really disgusted by him. It is important to remember that Swift and Pope were both sick men. Swift thought from time to time that he was going mad; 'I shall die like a tree at the top'. His actual illness, Ménière's syndrome, an affection of the inner ear which leads to giddiness, deafness, and nausea, does not lead to madness. Swift, an unusually long-lived man for his time, died of senile dementia, as we all may if we live long enough. Johnson in a poignant couplet has made eternally memorable the fate of great men who outlive both their talents and their senses:

From Marlb'rough's eyes the streams of dotage flow,
And Swift expires a driv'ler and a show.

Every day, in his later years, was for Pope a struggle with self-disgust and pain. The Dunciad, unlike the much gayer and more various Imitations of Horace, has, for Pope, a quality of 'visionary dreariness'. Even brilliant men grow weary in the sole occupation of writing. Fame had become a matter of stale habit. Many old friends were distant and dead, and making visits to great houses, when he was always demanding attention in the middle of the night, drams, coffee, ink, pens, paper, a weariness to him and his hosts. He was not even, if we can trust Spence, a very witty talker. The man was less amusing than the writer. Pope's own spleen and vapours seem to give the fourth book of The Dunciad, the vision of the triumph of Chaos, its melancholy power. Yet it contains his most powerful writing, and the complete new Dunciad was assembled in the year before his death, his last work, and perhaps his masterpiece. Paradoxically, we should be grateful to Cibber.

Sick as he was, Pope was actively preoccupied with writing till the end. He would have to leave publishing an edition of his complete collected works to Warburton, who produced it, in a handsome number of volumes, in 1751. He had said an emotional farewell on his death-bed to Bolingbroke, who had hidden his tears, and stammered out something about Pope's virtue. In 1749 Bolingbroke was to attack his old friend (though not fiercely, but with sad moderation) for printing more copies than Bolingbroke had permitted of The Patriot King and for having presumed to polish the text. Warburton made the only possible excuses. Pope's motives can hardly have been mercenary or corrupt; he admired his old friend's book excessively, wished it to circulate more widely, felt it had been composed in haste and might, in small things, be improved. Nothing can excuse breaking a promise; but Warburton sought at least to palliate Pope's offence. What is sad is that Pope had loved Bolingbroke more than all his friends, and Bolingbroke, in so far as such a self-centred man can love anybody, had loved him. By 1751, a lonely and sick Bolingbroke, the most brilliant failure of his time, was dead.

Pope had been born on 21 May 1688. He died on 30 May 1744, on the ninth day of his fifty-seventh year. The friends of his youth remained the friends of his painful last days. He had no real intention of cheating Bolingbroke. As the second Lady Bolingbroke, an intelligent Frenchwoman, observed, Pope was naturally generous and open-hearted but also naturally devious; with no great public affairs to occupy him, 'he played the politician about turnips and cabbages'. But there is a sadness about the aftermaths of a life devoted to friendship, when he was no longer alive to keep his friends together. Warburton was jealous of the generous provision Pope made for Martha Blount, or perhaps merely of Pope's love for her and recurrent praise of her in his poems. In his notes to his edition, he takes every opportunity to sneer at her in his heavy way. Yet, as we shall see later, even Warburton is forced to admit that the dying Pope had a strange burst of cheerfulness, a touch of new life, whenever Martha entered his room.

From 1709 to 1744, Pope had dominated English poetry. It is difficult to think of any other period in English poetry when one man had it all to himself. For an Eliot, there is always a Yeats; for a Tennyson, a Browning; for a Larkin, a Hughes. Some kind of reaction had to be expected, and the atmosphere of the time was also changing; the age of reason was becoming the age of sensibility. Even in the mid-eighteenth century Gray's quietly published *Elegy*, for all the firm Augustan morality that props its pensive sadness, hinted at the new note, and it is to be feared that Pope would have seen little in Collins's *Ode to Evening* or in the great vogue for collecting old ballads that began to make itself felt, through Ritson and Percy, at this time. He was not, as we shall see, without romantic feelings, to which in two poems at least he gave magnificent expression; but what appealed to him was the romance of human passion, not the romance of solitary musing, clouds and moonlight, ruined abbeys, and the hooting of the owl. If he has a limitation (and all great poets have their limitations) it is that he does not feel the charm of the vague, the distant, of what cannot exactly be defined.

He continued, nevertheless, to be the dominant poet of the century, the inspiring force behind Johnson, Goldsmith, and Crabbe; even Byron tried to write like Pope (very clumsily) in *English Bards and Scotch Reviewers* and praised him more than any other English poet.

But the Romantics were against him for lacking spontaneity and writing of artificial life, the Victorians for lack of a really deep seriousness and of their own special kind of strenuous exploratory thoughtfulness in verse. His fortune this century, though Dr Leavis has spoken up for him valiantly, is still uncertain. Under Eliot's influence, the attention of academic critics turned first to the Metaphysicals and then to the great argument about Milton. In reaction against Eliot, the Victorians have been receiving properly serious attention, and the Romantics will have their turn (Blake, Wordsworth, Keats, it may be said, have done so, but I do not know of a really rewarding book about the poetry – merely the poetry – of Coleridge, or about Shelley primarily as a poet).

The case is not quite similar with Pope. In the great Twickenham Edition he has attracted the finest efforts of modern scholarship (though, in their purely critical parts, the introductions vary in merit). There are excellent books about various aspects of his genius but, as my selective bibliography suggests, they are books by academics for academics.

I often think that one of our real difficulties with Pope is that the first half of the eighteenth century, when he flourished, though it is the period when we became, in the widest sense, a polite nation, and when the language of both verse and prose is as easy to read as any modern novel (much easier, indeed, than some) is yet a period oddly alien to us. When we read Boswell, we feel we are in a room with Johnson, Garrick, and the rest, talking to people we know. In the early part of the eighteenth century, the prose, the verse, is very natural, yet the naturalness seems to be playing a part.

However deeply we study Pope, for instance, we shall remain in some sort of doubt about what he really was like. But this is not only true of Pope, it is true (to take two extremes) of Addison and Bolingbroke. There is a tone of compliment and there is a tone of good-natured raillery. Are the compliments sincere? Is the raillery really good-natured? We worry about the cult of benevolence and virtue. We should be benevolent, of course, we should be virtuous, and we deserve some praise for it, since to be benevolent and virtuous is more merely than to do our duty. But any qualities that are talked about so much do cast doubt on how sincerely they are practised. Pope certainly practised the virtues, pursued reason (through submission to God), and was a true and loyal friend and expressed his friendship warmly. He expressed his spite warmly, also, and often with more memorable words. It is enough, perhaps, to say that unlike Yeats (who foolishly thought we could choose one or another) he knew that we cannot choose perfection in either our lives or works. He is a far greater poet than critics throughout a century-and-a-half allowed him to be. It is my belief that he was also a far better man. Of course, or he would not be human, he had his faults like the rest of us. But I count it to his credit that he says so little about his most obviously striking virtue, courage, cheerfulness, and sociability in the face of his daily and continual encounter with pain.

3

The Volume of 1717:
the Various Young Poet

In 1709, Pope (imitating Virgil, who had started off his career with his eclogues) published his four beautiful but extremely artificial *Pastorals*. His first important didactive poem, *An Essay on Criticism*, appeared in 1711 and, among many Restoration and Augustan poems about the nature of poetry – about nature or the poet's innate force as the source of poetry, and truth to nature as the main test of poetry (truth, especially, to human nature), about wit as the spur and judgment as the reins of Pegasus – this poem is the master work. In 1712, *Windsor Forest* showed powers of description even richer than those of the *Pastorals* and, in 1714, Pope published the revised and improved version of his greatest early poem, *The Rape of the Lock*. There had been other poems which appeared more to the taste of Pope's day than ours, the blending of Isaiah and Virgil's poem dedicated to Pollio which was often taken as a prophecy of the Incarnation and a rather stiff adaptation of Chaucer's *House of Fame*. Two new poems appeared in the 1717 volume, the powerful and still mysterious *Unfortunate Lady* and the Ovidian epistle, written with the departure of Lady Mary Wortley Montagu to Turkey in mind, *Eloisa to Abelard*. The modest and charming prose preface suggested that one of the few solid rewards of a gift for poetry was that it introduced the poet into good company. The volume, as a whole, though it had many passages of badinage and gaiety, was not the volume of a satirist; Pope half makes fun of fashionable life in *The Rape of the Lock* but part of him finds its elegant trivialities delightful. *An Essay on Criticism* has a few teasing lines on John Dennis (for which the fierce old critic never forgave Pope) but it is essentially didactic, and the qualities we notice in the *Pastorals* and *Windsor Forest* are a vivid sense of colour and a musicality which seem to look forward to Keats. *The Unfortunate Lady* and *Eloisa to Abelard* are the poems of a man of feeling, and even of a man of passion. If there is a certain artifice or convention in their expression of emotion, might not the same be said of the Romantics:

O Cuckoo! shall I call thee Bird
Or but a wandering Voice? . . .

Thou wast not born for death, immortal Bird! . . .

Hail to thee, blithe spirit!
Bird thou never wert . . .

Does it worry us that, from a prosaic point of view, Wordsworth's question is silly and Keats's and Shelley's statements untrue? We shall find it easier to get on with Pope if we permit him those poetic conventions which we permit, without question, to the poets of every other age.

Still, there is perhaps a very special artifice about Pope's *Pastorals*. There were, traditionally, two kinds of pastoral poetry, one typified by Marlow's idealistic picture of rustic love in 'The Passionate Shepherd to his Love' and the other by Sir Walter Ralegh's sardonic and bitter reply to it, on behalf of the shepherdess. Country life could be painted in fantastically beautiful colours, in elegant language, as if shepherds had nothing to do but woo and sing and the sheep looked after themselves. The lack of education, the narrow scope, of a life of rustic servitude could be ignored. Pope, in his early *Pastorals*, was fortunate enough to have a rival who aimed at the other kind of pastoral, the realistic pastoral, Ambrose Philips. Philips had given up a comfortable university fellowship to make a living and a reputation, as his friends Steele and Addison had done, as a poet and wit in London. He never forgave Pope for a smooth anonymous letter sent to Steele's *Guardian* which, quoting Philips at his most rustic and Pope himself at his most elegant, reproached Pope for mistaking the true nature of pastoral and deviating, if one compared him with the rough realism of Philips, 'into downright Poetry'. Yet it is quite possible that a modern reader might find this passage from Philips's *Second Pastoral*, which expresses not the imaginary feelings of an ideal shepherd, but the disappointments that the pursuit first of learning, then of poetry have brought to Philips, much more true to human feeling than Pope:

COLINET

Small need there was, in random search of gain,
To drive my pining flock athward the plain,

31

To distant *Cam*. Fine gain at length, I trow,
To hoard up to myself such deal of woe!
My sheep quite spent, through travel and ill-fare,
And, like their keeper, ragged grown and bare;
The damp, cold greensward, for my nightly bed,
And some slant willow's trunk to rest my head.
Hard is to bear of pinching cold the pain,
And hard is want to the unpractised swain:
But neither want, nor pinching cold, is hard,
To blasting storms of calumny compared!
Unkind as hail it falls; the pelting shower
Destroys the tender herb and budding flower.

Poor Philips was born a little earlier than Pope in 1675 and died a little later in 1749. After Pope's smoothly satirical article in Steele's *Guardian* he hung up a cudgel in Button's coffee-house to beat Pope should he ever dare appear. But if not calumny at least mockery pursued his life and his poems for children, in which he was a pioneer, earned him the mocking nickname of 'Namby-Pamby'. After Queen Anne's death in 1714, Addison's influence rescued him from poverty and got him several posts in Ireland; 'ambiguous gifts, as what gods give must be', for Ireland was generally considered, as by Swift when he was given the Deanery of St Patrick's, a place of cultural exile. It makes Philips's case all the sadder that he could write, as in the lines I have quoted, with a certain power.

Pope, in his own *Pastorals*, aims not at power but at elegance. The delicious introduction to the second Pastoral, 'on Summer', addressed to his friend, Dr Garth, the author of *The Dispensary*, are not those of a young man who has actually felt the passion of love:

Accept, O *Garth*, the Muse's early lays,
That adds this Wreath of Ivy to thy Bays;
Hear what from Love unpractis'd Hearts endure,
From Love, the sole Disease thou canst not cure!
Ye shady Beeches, and ye cooling Streams,
Defence from *Phoebus'*, not from *Cupid's* Beams;
To you I mourn; nor to the Deaf I sing,
The Woods shall answer, and their Echo ring.
The Hills and Rocks attend my doleful Lay,
Why art thou prouder and more hard than they?
The bleating Sheep with my Complaints agree,

They parch'd with Heat, and I inflam'd by thee.
The sultry *Sirius* burns his thirsty Plains,
While in thy Heart Eternal Winter reigns.

We find ourselves searching, among these airs and graces, for the object actually seen. And Pope, after Keats the most pictorial of all English poets, does not disappoint us:

Here the bright Crocus and blue Vi'let glow;
Here Western Winds on breathing Roses blow . . .

Behold the *Groves* that shine with silver Frost,
Their Beauty wither'd, and their Verdure lost . . .

Yet it is to *Windsor Forest* that we should turn for Pope's brightest colours. More memorable in the *Pastorals* is his beauty of cadence, as in the Third Pastoral, that dedicated to Autumn, where Pope offers us something like the conclusion of Milton's *Lycidas*, but smoothed and simplified for an Augustan audience:

Thus sung the Shepherds till th'Approach of Night,
The Skies yet blushing with departing Light,
When falling Dews with Spangles deck'd the Glade,
And the low Sun had lengthen'd ev'ry Shade.

Nevertheless, in developing the vein of the *Pastorals*, *Windsor Forest* (first intended as a tribute to Sir William Trumbull, the young Pope's companion in forest rides, and finally dedicated to Lansdowne who was not only a grander personage but had a more euphonious name) displays the young Pope's genius more clearly to a modern reader. The *Pastorals* are in a sense the most marvellous example of Pope's juvenilia: Pope had been working on them, and asking advice on them, since 1704. In *Windsor Forest* we see Pope's painterly skill at its grandest:

See! from the Brake the whirring Pheasant springs,
And mounts exulting on triumphant Wings;
Short is his Joy! he feels the fiery Wound,
Flutters in Blood, and panting beats the Ground.
Ah! What avail his glossie, varying Dyes,
His Purple Crest, and Scarlet-circled Eyes,
The vivid Green his shining Plumes unfold;
His painted Wings, and Breast that flames with Gold!

But *Windsor Forest* was not a poem where, in a phrase of Pope's own

33

from *An Epistle to Dr Arbuthnot*, 'pure Description held the place of Sense'. The signing of the Treaty of Utrecht (attended by the fall of Marlborough and the rise to power of Pope's Tory friends, Henry St John, Viscount Bolingbroke, and Robert Harley, Earl of Oxford and Earl Mortimer) gave Pope the chance for a great invocation to the Thames, which flows through Windsor Forest, as a future channel of peaceful trade which will unite Great Britain prosperously and happily with all the countries of the world (it is typical of a certain lack in Pope of the coherent large view that, when England got a great peace Minister, Sir Robert Walpole, Pope, loyal to his old friends thrust from power, hated him):

> Thy Trees, fair *Windsor*! now shall leave their Woods,
> And half thy Forests rush into my Floods,
> Bear *Britain*'s Thunder, and her Cross display,
> To the bright Regions of the rising Day;
> Tempt Icy Seas, where scarce the Waters Roll,
> Where clearer Flames glow round the frozen Pole;
> Or under Southern Skies exalt their Sails,
> Led by new Stars, and born by spicy Gales!
> For me the Balm shall bleed, and Amber flow,
> The Coral redden, and the Ruby glow,
> The Pearly Shell its lucid Globe infold,
> And *Phoebus* warm the ripening Ore to Gold.

It is the personified Thames, of course, addressing Windsor Forest and Pope, the laureate of peace, enchanting the reader with a vision of future richness and harmony:

> The Time shall come, when free as Seas or Wind
> Unbounded *Thames* shall flow for all Mankind,
> Whole Nations enter with each swelling Tyde,
> And Seas but join the Regions they divide;
> Earth's distant Ends our Glory shall behold,
> And the new World launch forth to seek the Old.

The Thames looks forward to the strange prospect of Red Indian chiefs exploring its banks:

> Then Ships of uncouth Form shall stem the Tyde,
> And Feather'd People crowd my wealthy Side,
> And naked Youths and painted Chiefs admire
> Our Speech, our Colour, and our strange Attire!

Pope ends on a note of exultation, in which free commercial intercourse is seen as the destruction of tyranny (particularly, for his Catholicism never affected his patriotism, of the rule of the Spaniards and Portuguese in Latin America):

> On stretch thy Reign, fair *Peace*! from Shore to Shore,
> Till Conquest cease, and Slav'ry be no more:
> Till the freed *Indians* in their native Groves
> Reap their own Fruits, and woo their Sable Loves,
> *Peru* once more a Race of Kings behold,
> And other *Mexico's* be roof'd with Gold.
> Exil'd by Thee from Earth to deepest Hell,
> In Brazen Bonds shall barb'rous *Discord* dwell:
> Gigantick *Pride*, pale *Terror*, gloomy *Care*,
> And mad *Ambition*, shall attend her there.
> There purple *Vengeance* bath'd in Gore retires,
> Her Weapons blunted, and extinct her Fires:
> There hateful *Envy* her own Snakes shall feel,
> And *Persecution* mourn her broken Wheel:
> There *Faction* roar, *Rebellion* bite her chain,
> And gasping Furies thirst for Blood in vain.

Peace, though the greatest public blessing of mankind, has rarely been treated in verse with heroic splendour: here Pope – though, as always, we must adjust ourselves to the tone, oddly alien to us, of his period – succeeds in that arduous and noble task.

I have taken the *Pastorals* and *Windsor Forest* together because, in spite of the gap in the time of composition, the second can be considered as the maturation of the first. The great didactic poem of the 1717 volume, *An Essay on Criticism*, now deserves our attention. It is not important for originality; every thought in it is a commonplace, and often a shallow one, of the criticism of Pope's time. It is not a masterpiece of construction. Pope lacked the gift of what Dryden called 'sequaciousness' and was short-winded in argument. His poems were often tessellated together out of short passages scribbled on the backs of letters or other used scraps of paper. (T. S. Eliot, except that he used a notebook rather than old letters and envelopes, composed in rather the same way; short passages came to him spontaneously; the problem of composition, at least in Eliot's early work, was that of fitting the scraps together into something that had meaning and impact as a whole. It is worth adding, perhaps, that the personalities of these two great poets are mysterious in a somewhat similar way. With both poets, as we read their verses with growing astonishment and admiration, the man within the name is as elusive as he is omnipresent.)

As sometimes in early Eliot, then, in *An Essay on Criticism* of 1711, the parts are more striking than the whole. Yet, as we shall see, just as *Windsor Forest* celebrates the Augustan idea (literary Augustan, for it was the idea of Julius Caesar's heir and successor, the Emperor Augustus) of an empire of universal peace and prosperity, so *An Essay on Criticism* celebrates the idea of great literature and humane thought as the marks of a new universal civilisation and, in spite of Pope's Catholicism, rejects the Middle Ages as a 'Gothick' and barbarous time. Pope's Christianity is that of the great moderate man, the defender of sound scholarship and good sense, of the Renaissance: the Christian humanism of the Renaissance. And literature and sensibility have really no models for him except in the ancient Mediterranean world and in Renaissance and post-Renaissance Europe. Such general ideas as he has are those of Aristotle, as Aristotle was distorted, either by simplification or over-elaboration, by Renaissance critics.

An Essay on Criticism is, thus, less worth reading for its general ideas (Pope was never a powerful or original thinker) than for its illustrations of them. Thus Pope tells us that to read poetry for the sound not for the sense is like going to church not for the doctrine but for the music. The point is sharply made, but it is its illustrations that are brilliant:

> But most by *Numbers* judge a Poet's Song,
> And *smooth* or *rough* with them, is *right* or *wrong*;
> In the bright *Muse* tho' thousand *Charms* conspire,
> Her *Voice* is all these tuneful Fools admire,
> Who haunt *Parnassus* but to please their Ear,
> Not mend their Minds; as some to *Church* repair,
> Not for the *Doctrine*, but the *Musick* there.
> These *Equal Syllables* alone require,
> Tho' oft the Ear the *open Vowels* tire,
> While *Expletives* their feeble Aid *do* join,
> And ten low Words oft creep in one dull Line,
> While they ring round the same *unvary'd Chimes*,
> With sure *Returns* of still *expected Rhymes*,
> Where-e'er you find *the cooling Western Breeze*,
> In the next Line, it *whispers thro' the Trees*;

If *Chrystal Streams with pleasing Murmurs creep*,
The Reader's threaten'd (not in vain) with *Sleep*.
Then, at the *last* and *only* Couplet fraught
With some *unmeaning* Thing they call a *Thought*,
A *needless Alexandrine* ends the Song,
That like a wounded Snake, drags its slow length along.

What worried some of the recusant Catholic gentry (particularly
one of Pope's most loved and trusted friends, John Caryll, who had
introduced the young Pope to Theresa and Martha Blount) were certain lines in *An Essay on Man* which seemed as sharp as any Protestant
could be in their attack on the ignorance and bigotry, not of Catholicism as such, but of medieval or pre-Reformation Catholicism. They
were lines like this:

Once *School-Divines* this zealous Isle o'erspread;
Who knew most *Sentences* was *deepest read*:
Faith, Gospel, All, seem'd made to be *disputed*,
And none had *Sense enough to be Confuted*.
Scotists and *Thomists*, now, in Peace remain,
Amidst their *Kindred Cobwebs* in *Duck-Lane*.

Duck Lane, near Smithfield, was full of second-hand bookstalls. Pope,
of course, could not be expected to foresee what Duns Scotus would
mean to a great poet like Hopkins or how the revival of interest in
logic in our own time would lead to a close and respectful study of the
scholastics by critical and innovatory logicians like Professor Peter
Geach. But Caryll feared that such passages might lead to bad feeling
among Pope's co-religionists, as might the passage leading up to Pope's
eulogium of Erasmus:

Thus long succeeding Criticks justly reign'd,
Licence repress'd, and *useful Laws* ordain'd:
Learning and *Rome* alike in Empire grew,
And *Arts* still *follow'd* where her *Eagles* flew;
From the same Foes, at last, both felt their Doom,
And the same Age saw *Learning* fall, and *Rome*.
With Tyranny, then *Superstition* join'd
As that the *Body*, this enslav'd the *Mind*; . . .
A *second* Deluge Learning thus o'er run
And the *Monks* finish'd what the *Goths* begun.
At length, *Erasmus*, that *great, injur'd* Name,

(The *Glory* of the Priesthood, and the *Shame!*)
Stemm'd the *wild Torrent* of a *barb'rous Age*,
And drove those *Holy Vandals* off the Stage.

Caryll was wrong in thinking that Pope's insistence on the scholarship
and reasonableness of Erasmian Catholicism would, in fact, offend
English Roman Catholics who, after their troubles in the Popish plot,
were in spirit ecumenical: more anxious to insist on the values that
united them to their Anglican brethren, and on their essentially obedient and law-abiding patriotism, than on the doctrines that still held
them apart. The Augustan age was one which, in all Christian bodies,
was insisting on the reasonableness of true religion, on what united
Christians, not what divided them. Answering Caryll, Pope made his
own point of view very clear:

> I've ever thought the best piece of service one could do to our
> religion was to expose our detestation and scorn of all those
> artifices and *piae fraudes* which it stands so little in need of, and
> which have laid it under so great a scandal among the enemies.
> Nothing has been so much a scarecrow to them as the too
> peremptory and seemingly uncharitable assertion of an utter
> impossibility of salvation to all but ourselves, invincible ignorance
> excepted . . . Besides the small number of the truly faithful in our
> Church, we must again subdivide, and the Jansenist is damned by
> the Jesuit, the Jesuit by the Jansenist, the strict Scotist by the
> Thomist, etc. There may be errors, I grant, but I can't think 'em
> of such consequence as to destroy utterly the charity of mankind,
> the very greatest bond in which we are engaged by God to one
> another . . .

This is the tone and feeling of the modern ecumenical movement. And
even in the strictly critical parts of *An Essay on Man* there is a sense of
Nature as a quasi-Divine power, rather like Coleridge's sense of Imagination in *Biographia Literaria*, published in 1815, a century after Pope's
youthful didactic masterpiece of 1711:

> First follow NATURE, and your Judgment frame
> By her just standard, which is still the same:
> *Unerring Nature*, still divinely bright,
> One *clear, unchang'd* and *Universal* Light,
> At once the *Source,* and *End,* and *Test* of *Art.*
> *Art* from that Fund each *just Supply* provides,

Works *without Show*, and *without Pomp* presides:
In some fair Body thus th' informing Soul
With Spirits feeds, with Vigour fills the whole,
Each Motion guides, and ev'ry Nerve sustains;
It self unseen, but in th' *Effects* remains.

Thus Nature, for Pope, is very much what Coleridge in 'Dejection: An Ode' calls 'the shaping spirit of Imagination'. The great Augustan and the great Romantic are at one in their sense of the sources.

Caryll had probably been not really profoundly distressed by Pope's treatment of the Middle Ages. The revived taste for the 'Gothick' (apart from comic treatments of the medieval, or rather of Spenser's mock-medieval style, as by Thomson in *The Castle of Indolence*) really belongs to the second half of the century, the years after Pope's death. Caryll's real worry had been about the danger of the Catholic recusant families, a small and self-defensively coherent group, being divided among themselves. Two such families, the Fermors and the family of Lord Petre, had been estranged from each other by a foolish incident in which, intending a gesture of gallantry, Lord Petre had cut off a lock of Arabella Fermor's beautiful hair. Caryll felt that by treating the whole incident light-heartedly, in a mock-heroic vein, Pope would laugh the two ancient families out of their unnecessary feud about what was not a deliberate act of insolence but a misplaced piece of playfulness. Pope saw an opportunity to display his natural taste and delicacy (the qualities which differentiate the early Augustan period from the sometimes more vigorous but often coarse and violent period of the Restoration) and to indulge the natural gaiety which seems, in spite of the early onslaughts of invalidism, to have marked his character until, after thirty, he immersed himself in solidity and Homer. The first version of *The Rape of the Lock*, a fairly short one, without the later addition of the marvellous epic machinery of sylphs and gnomes (it was part of Pope's case against Addison that he advised against the addition) was sent to the publishers in 1712. The revised and enlarged version appeared in 1714. *The Rape of the Lock* is generally recognised as, if not the greatest, at least the most perfect of Pope's early poems.

Pope's object throughout (as he put it to Spence, a dull but useful anecdotist, to whom we owe most of the records we have of Pope's conversation) was 'to make a jest of it, and laugh [the two families] together again'. It had the desired effect. One might have expected Arabella Fermor, the Belinda of the poem, to be slightly resentful; but

D

if Pope hints that Belinda is a slightly silly girl he makes it very clear that she is an extraordinarily attractive one, and Arabella was very ready to accept the prose dedication of the enlarged edition. He was, in this enlarged edition, able to indulge his taste for the pretty and fanciful with the supernatural machinery of the protective sylphs, which he had found in a French Rosicrucian romance. (It is odd that he shared an interest in the Rosicrucians with the great poet least like him in our language, William Butler Yeats. But Pope's magic, unlike Yeats's, is all elegance and pretence.)

One should make a sharp distinction between the mock-heroic, the treatment of trivial episodes in noble language, which is the *genre* of *The Rape of the Lock*, and the burlesque, the treatment of traditionally noble events in low language and a mocking mood, which is the *genre* of Samuel Butler's *Hudibras* and, in part at least, of that complex work, Joyce's *Ulysses*. The first *genre* appeals to more delicate spirits. Perhaps, however, the poets who wrote mock-epics in both styles were directing what satire was really part of these broad or high comedy poems to the universal mechanical praise of Homer and the 'receipts to make an epic' extracted from his Renaissance commentators by critics who perhaps (like Pope himself, who was to become a great translator of Homer) hardly knew any Greek. Pope took advantage of the chance to expand the poem not merely to fit in the sylph machinery and the Cave of Spleen, the mock supernatural element, but to produce something that was more like a real epic in elegant miniature. The satire is directed against the form, not against the subject-matter; Pope found the world of the grand mode agreeable enough, and the different sort of pleasant absurdity of the sylphs a good brilliant diminishing mirror, like that over Belinda's dressing-table, for Belinda's world of important trifles. Geoffrey Tillotson, in his notes on *The Rape of the Lock* in the preface to the Twickenham Edition, shrewdly remarks that Aubrey Beardsley's illustrations seem to suit the poem exactly because, like it, they are 'filigree work'.

Yet the ornate and graceful fantastication of the trifling, which is what we remember most about *The Rape of the Lock*, does not mean that the poem is not, like all Pope's poems, packed with sound moral sense. One might quote Clarissa's wise speech, which is also, in its urbanely grave way, high poetry, from the beginning of Canto V:

Say, why are Beauties prais'd and honour'd most,
The wise Man's Passion, and the vain Man's Toast?

Why deck'd with all that Land and Sea afford,
Why Angels call'd, and Angel-like ador'd?
Why round our Coaches crowd the white-glov'd Beaus,
Why bows the Side-box from its inmost Rows?
How vain are all these Glories, all our Pains,
Unless good Sense preserve what Beauty gains:
That Men may say, when we the Front-box grace,
Behold the first in Virtue, as in Face!
Oh! if to dance all Night, and dress all Day,
Charm'd the Small-pox, or chas'd old Age away;
Who would not scorn what Huswife's Cares produce,
Or who would learn one earthly Thing of Use?
To patch, nay ogle, might become a Saint,
Nor could it sure be such a Sin to paint.
But since, alas! frail Beauty must decay,
Curl'd or uncurl'd, since Locks will turn to grey,
Since painted, or not painted, all shall fade,
And she who scorns a Man, must die a Maid;
What then remains, but well our Pow'r to use,
And keep good Humour still whate'er we lose?
And trust me, Dear! good Humour can prevail,
When airs, and Flights, and Screams, and Scolding fail.
Beauties in vain their pretty Eyes may roll;
Charms strike the Sight, but Merit wins the Soul.

Pope had created an almost self-contained world as delicate as gossamer yet as strong as a net of tensile steel wires. The world of *The Rape of the Lock* is self-contained, transcends and transforms the actual. Pope was oddly annoyed when the real Arabella Fermor made a perfectly sensible and respectable marriage. He would have liked her preserved for ever in the inaccessible beauty of Belinda, Belinda with her dressing-table scattered with Bibles and *billets-doux*, with the cross hanging between her lovely breasts which '*Jews* might kiss, and Infidels adore'.

The Rape of the Lock is certainly the most original and by general judgment the most successful of the poems of the 1717 volume. I think I have indicated the very limited and special sense in which this good-humoured masterpiece could be called a satire. There is an element of general satire, on foolish critics and bad poets, of course, in *An Essay on Criticism*, but it is essentially a didactic poem. There are, in fact, four lines of personal satire, directed against the critic and dramatist, John

Dennis, to whom the young Pope had been introduced by Wycherley. The 'squab' little gentleman, in his plain country clothes, was taken by Dennis for the son of one of Wycherley's tenants in the country and when the little man presumed to argue with the great John Dennis, Dennis (by no means a negligible critic, whose dissection of Addison's over-praised *Cato* is still worth reading as a vigorous example of well-reasoned destructive criticism) snubbed the young man unmercifully. At no time in his life was Pope the man to put up with a snub. His lines on Dennis are memorable: Pope is making the sound point that critical discussion should be easy, free, and polite. The reference to Dennis would be made clear to contemporary readers by the indirect reference to the failure of Dennis's tragedy *Appius and Virginia* and the over-fondness of Dennis in verse for the adjective 'tremendous'. The reference to the tyrant in old tapestry makes the irascible elderly critic seem both inhumane and unreal; he is a mere tattered Gothic image whose threats can be safely ignored: ,

'Twere well, might Criticks still this Freedom take;
But *Appius* reddens at each Word you speak,
And *stares, Tremendous*! with a *threatening Eye*
Like some *fierce Tyrant* in *Old Tapestry*!

Dennis had a reputation at this time as a senior critic somewhere between those of Mr Grigson and Dr Leavis today. He was feared but respected as a severe critic, but, according to his own lights and the lights of the day, also as a learned and just one. The feelings of compunction that the young should always feel in rebuking the elderly ought to have restrained Pope; and established reputation deserves to be treated by the young with a certain deference, however shaky they may feel its foundations to be. (Dennis's friends included not only Wycherley but the most esteemed writer of the age, the master of English comedy, William Congreve.) Pope must have felt slightly guilty for, in spite of much provocation from Dennis, he remained mild about him even after the beginning of Pope's properly satirical period, beginning with *The Dunciad* in 1728; and, when Dennis was old and poor, Pope generously wrote a preface for a benefit performance of one of his plays, praising Dennis's sturdy, obstinate English virtues. (The benefit night of a play was the third night, whose profits accrued solely to the author. This is one of those many generous and forgiving acts of Pope's which one might admire a little more if the author did not call so much attention to them himself.)

Of the other poems in the 1717 volume, two, published there for the first time, demand special attention. One is the most mysterious and in some ways the most moving poem Pope ever wrote, hinting at a wider and deeper range of feeling than Pope ever exhibited with the same conciseness, before and after; and yet exasperating in the way the nature of the story is almost deliberately blurred and obscured. We know that the poem was inspired by the misfortunes of two ladies, a Mrs Cope and a Mrs Weston, in whom Pope took a sympathetic interest; but we know little of them, except that neither committed suicide, as the lady in the poem appears to have done, for reasons that Pope leaves portentously and irritatingly vague.

One might say that it would have been a great poem, it has great lines and passages, if only Pope had left us enough clues to know what it is about – if the lady, for instance, loved below or above her station, if she loved a married man or was forbidden by a guardian to marry a single man whom her guardian found unsuitable, or was forced into an unsuitable marriage though she loved somebody other than her bridegroom. The poem falls into moral absurdity by saying that if 'eternal justice rules the ball', the guardian's descendants will die in a similarly tragic way. The guardian's descendants have no responsibility for the lady's misfortunes and a God who punished them for her misfortunes would be very unjust. Pope's usual sanity and judgment have deserted him. He is carried away by emotions which he either did not fully understand himself, or did not dare to explore fully. Yet this is the most powerful of his shorter poems.

It contains near the beginning a passage that (as Middleton Murry first noticed) might have been written by a Donne with a taste for smoother versification:

Most souls, 'tis true, but peep out once an age,
Dull sullen pris'ners in the body's cage:
Dim lights of life that burn a length of years,
Useless, unseen, as lamps in sepulchres;
Like Eastern Kings a lazy state they keep,
And close confin'd to their own palace sleep.

The resemblance is not intended, nor is one's sense of it a fancy. It is not simply that one is remembering Donne's

And as in Tullia's tomb one lamp burnt clear
For more than fifteen hundred year . . .

43

These lines are exactly what T. S. Eliot admired in the Metaphysicals: an undissociated sensibility, a fusion of thought and feeling, though occurring from Eliot's point of view at exactly the wrong period. But the variety of style in the short poem is extraordinary; any admirer of the Romantics would be delighted by these lines:

What tho' no sacred earth allow thee room,
Nor hallow'd dirge be mutter'd o'er thy tomb?
Yet shall thy grave with rising flow'rs be drest,
And the green turf lie lightly on thy breast:
There shall the morn her earliest tears bestow,
There the first roses of the year shall blow . . .

As a devout Christian, Dr Johnson was shocked by the way the poem treats suicide as a noble and heroic act. But with his extraordinary critical fairness, he admitted that the lines must 'be allowed to be written in some parts, with vigorous animation, and in others with gentle tenderness; nor has Pope produced any poem in which the sense predominates more over the diction.' In our own time, Professor Graham Hough has examined four extremely obscure lines and asked whether their obscurity may not be part of their strength (see 'An Eighth Type of Ambiguity', in *William Empson, The Man and His Work*, edited by Roma Gill, Routledge & Kegan Paul, London, 1974, pp. 89–90).

The lines Professor Hough chooses for pregnant and powerful obscurity are these:

How lov'd, how honour'd once, avails thee not,
To whom related, or by whom begot;
A heap of dust alone remains of thee;
'Tis all thou art, and all the proud shall be.

Professor Hough points out that these lines, for all their look of balanced clarity, are (and apparently deliberately) baffling. We are not given clues whether they deal with a now deceased girl very much loved but not honoured, very much honoured but not loved, both loved and honoured; had she low relations but a distinguished father (perhaps she was illegitimate?), or distinguished relations but an unfortunate parentage (perhaps her father or her mother had married beneath his or her station or above it?) Was she one of 'the proud', the nobly born or connected? Or has she indeed such a high rank but such a high spirit that she disdained her high rank? Or was there some stain in her birth that excluded her from 'the proud' (yet they will be no better off than she in the end)?

Professor Hough rightly points out that if these lines were clearer they would not be so powerful or so painfully self-revealing. Pope himself was torn all his life by ambiguous feelings about 'the proud'. There was a feeling that it was better to be a virtuous man than to be a great poet, and better to be either than to be a mere fine gentleman (the sort of elegant trifler depicted, say, in Sir Plume in *The Rape of the Lock*). But there was another feeling that unless one was accepted fully as a fine gentleman (and it would be more because of one's poetry than one's virtue), life for a crippled dwarf in continual pain would be unbearable.

For a passionate man like Pope, also, virtue, the equable sense of justice, can too easily be turned by blinding rage into its opposite:

Cold is that breast which warm'd the world before,
And those love-darting eyes must roll no more.
Thus, if eternal justice rules the ball,
Thus shall your wives and thus your children fall:
On all the line a sudden vengeance waits,
And frequent hearses shall besiege your gates.

These lines are certainly written with 'vigorous animation' but nobody would describe them as expressing the sentiments of a virtuous or perhaps a wholly sane man. The *Elegy to the Memory of an Unfortunate Lady*, for Pope a comparatively short poem (about two and a half pages in most editions), nevertheless tells us more about the deep and painful springs of feeling in Pope than anything else he has written. In its vindictive tenderness it displays the preference of the true poet for what Lionel Trilling calls the authentic (the feelings that drive a young woman deprived of her lover to rebellious suicide) to what he calls the sincere (the patient and resigned acceptance of disappointment which Pope, in a moralising mood, would himself have counselled). It is authenticity in Trilling's sense rather than sincerity that gives the true poet his lawless power.

Eloisa to Abelard, inspired by Lady Mary Wortley Montagu's departure for Turkey, is modelled on Ovid's *Heroides* or letters from classical heroines to their absent husbands or lovers, and is a smoother, clearer, more artful poem than the *Unfortunate Lady* but not springing from such deep or genuine feelings. Abelard, the most brilliant schoolman of his day in Paris, had been asked by Canon Fulbert to give private tutorials to the Canon's clever but very attractive bluestocking niece, Eloisa. Abelard, so far as we know, was a most conscientious tutor but, of course, he took the opportunity to seduce his pupil, nor was she at all unwilling. Both, at this stage, were interested in the application of the new logic to such philosophic propositions as could be deduced from Christian dogma, not in the least in the Christian life. Canon Fulbert got wind of the affair and had Abelard castrated by a couple of ruffians. Forsaking logic and Eloisa, Abelard started a spiritual retreat called the Paraclete; Eloisa became an Abbess, devout and a strict disciplinarian. They began to correspond, and the old feelings caught fire again. Sexual potency was not in Abelard a necessary or even central element in the passion of love, and the need for Abelard, which Eloisa felt reviving in herself, burned all the more because it could never be physically satisfied. Both struggled, but at moments almost hopelessly, to make a gift of their renewed passion to God; it was Abelard who thought it wiser to break off the correspondence. *Eloisa to Abelard* is a fascinating poem in its psychological acuteness in exploring Eloisa's inner life, the various ways in which images and memories and longings for Abelard interrupt her attempts to concentrate on God. F. W. Bateson thinks it a wax-work poem but Eloisa seems to me a more real and complexly conceived person than, let us say, Madeline in Keats's *The Eve of St Agnes*. Pope would beat most Romantic and Victorian poets on their own ground of exploration of the inner self as well as his own special ground of Ovidian facility and neatness.

Yet one sees why some readers have felt the emotion a little self-indulgent and even sickly. Pope turns the conclusion of the poem to a dedication and to a (slightly concealed) declaration of love for Lady Mary. One reflects that she was, for all her fine looks in youth, a mannish sort of woman (she doted on an effeminate but very handsome young Italian, Algarotti, who also attracted, with no ill feeling between the two rivals, her friend Lord Hervey). Unconsciously, Pope is giving Lady Mary the active role and himself Eloisa's passive feminine role of passionate but hopeless expectation. Such a confusion of sexual fantasy-roles was bound to end in humiliation for Pope, and his 'love' for Lady Mary turned later with alarming rapidity to obscene hatred. We read the conclusion of the poem, with all this in mind, but also with its own tone in mind, feeling it does not ring quite true:

If ever chance two wandering lovers brings

To *Paraclete*'s white walls, and silver springs,
O'er the pale marble shall they join their heads,
And drink the falling tears each other sheds;
Then sadly say, with mutual pity moved,
'Oh may we never love as these have loved!'
From the full quire when loud *Hosannas* rise,
And swell the pomp of dreadful sacrifice,
Amid that scene, if some relenting eye
Glance on the stone where our cold relics lie,
Devotion's self shall steal a thought from heav'n,
One human tear shall drop, and be forgiv'n.
And sure if fate some future Bard shall join
In sad similitude of griefs to mine,
Condemn'd whole years in absence to deplore,
And image charms he must behold no more,
Such if there be, who loves so long, so well;
Let him our sad, our tender story tell;
The best-sung woes will soothe my pensive ghost;
He best can paint 'em who shall feel 'em most.

Lulled though we are by the smooth artifice of the verse, we still know (and Pope knows) that the part of the romantic lover lies outside his very extensive repertoire; and if the tone is not quite sincere nor the feelings quite authentic, the longing to play the part that nature has forbidden is real enough.

The preface to the 1717 volume contrasts in its urbanity and ease with these two disturbing poems. No poet as great as Pope has ever, so far as I know, made such sane and moderate claims for the advantages (and there are real advantages) to be derived from the possession and the acknowledged reputation of true poetic talent:

There are indeed some advantages accruing from a Genius to Poetry, and they are all I can think of: the agreeable power of self-amusement when a man is idle or alone; the privilege of being admitted into the best company; and the freedom of saying as many careless things as other people, without being so severely remark'd upon.

I am not sure that the sane cheerfulness of Pope's temperament might not be the most lingering impression that the volume of 1717 left with his more intelligent readers. Not among the greatest but among the most charming things are little poems for the Miss Blounts (not directly to Martha, but to Theresa as the elder sister): this *amitié amoureuse* was the kind of lively and undemanding friendship with a woman for which Pope was physically and temperamentally suited, and after the strained striking of romantic attitudes to Lady Mary we feel here that we are in a world of personal and social realities, as in *Epistle to Miss Blount, with the Works of Voiture*,

> Let the strict Life of graver Mortals be
> A long, exact, and serious Comedy,
> In ev'ry Scene some Moral let it teach,
> And, if it can, at once both Please and Preach,
> Let mine, an innocent gay Farce appear,
> And more Diverting still than Regular . . .

Even more full of the hearty jollities of life is Pope's *Epistle to Miss Blount, on her leaving the Town, after the Coronation*, with its vivid picture (one is reminded of Mrs Sullen in Farquhar's *The Beaux' Stratagem*) of country boredoms following hard on the heels of city pleasures:

> She went, to plain-work, and to purling brooks,
> Old-fashion'd halls, dull aunts, and croaking rooks,
> She went from Op'ra, park, assembly, play,
> To morning walks, and pray'rs three hours a day;
> To pass her time 'twixt reading and Bohea,
> To muse, and spill her solitary Tea,
> Or o'er cold coffee trifle with the spoon,
> Count the slow clock, and dine exact at noon;
> Divert her eyes, with pictures in the fire,
> Hum half a tune, tell stories to the squire;
> Up to her godly garret after sev'n,
> There starve and pray, for that's the way to heav'n.
>   Some Squire, perhaps, you take delight to rack,
> Whose game is Whisk, whose treat a toast in sack;
> Who visits with a gun, presents you birds,
> Then gives a smacking buss, and cries – No words!
> Or with his hound comes hollowing from the stable,
> Makes love with nods, and knees beneath a table;
> Whose laughs are hearty, tho' his jests are coarse,
> And loves you best of all things – but his horse.

The ease and naturalness of the manner there looks forward to the greatest eighteenth-century comic novelist, Henry Fielding, one of Pope's warmest admirers. Alas, as we shall see in the next chapter, ten years of growing illness and of agonising labours upon Homer were to send the gay young spark off the stage for ever; Pope was to remain a great poet, but of a quite different kind.

4

Pope and Homer

Since classical times there have been doubts about Homer. Were the texts we possess actually written down by a historical Homer or orally transmitted through his bardic disciples, the Homerides, and reduced to writing (in a diction as archaic to Plato and Aristotle, say, as Chaucer or even pre-Chaucerian medieval verse to ourselves) a good many years after his death? Did Homer write or orally compose the *Iliad* and the *Odyssey* at a time roughly contemporary with the period he writes about, when Greece was a loose confederation of tribal kingdoms, or three or four hundred years after? There is much in the poem that the poet does not seem fully to understand himself. It would seem that the use of chariots in warfare had fallen out of use in his own time. In his works, he sometimes uses chariots as places from which warriors can fling spears but more usually they deposit warriors on the battlefield for single combat on foot and are not used rationally. This is in contrast to the Celtic chariots which Caesar describes vividly so much later in his account of his tactical reconnaissance of the southern shores of our island. The site of Troy was, of course, discovered by Schliemann, but it was a city on a key trade route that had been invaded many times and in his amateurish eagerness Schliemann dug right through Homer's Troy.

The general opinion seems to be that there was a single poet called Homer, who was the master of at least some sort of writing, who composed his poems with recitation in mind, and did not improvise them from traditional material as he went along. There was a great deal of traditional material, like Scottish ballad material, which Homer was using; but both his poems have more complexity and unity than a set of traditional ballads run together would have had and, in spite of their use of set formulas of phrase and episode, have a unity that could be stamped on them by one man's creative skill and imagination, and only by that. At the same time, it is true that there tend to be inconsistencies between different accounts of the same event such as we expect in orally transmitted literature, and that in some ways the *Iliad*, 'the poem of force' as Simone Weil called it, and the essential romantic *Odyssey* with its marvels and surprises (Circe and her magic powers of transformation, the Sirens, the Cyclops, the whole final episode of the apparent beggar Odysseus slaying the suitors) appeal to quite different emotions; one is tragic, the other a good tale of adventure with much magic in it. Some critics have thought that the *Iliad* and the *Odyssey* must therefore have two different authors (the *Odyssey* an authoress according to Samuel Butler, corresponding roughly to Nausicaa, the hospitable king's daughter in the tale). The general belief now, however, is in a single Homer. Many of these problems did not, of course, exist for Pope. The problem that did exist for him was that it was morally impossible for him to see Homer's world as a remote and barbarous one and his art also, like the art of the ballad, as having a certain primitive roughness. The characters must behave and express themselves with the aristocratic elegance of Pope's own time. One of Homer's most distinctive qualities, the quality of epic monotony (Achilles always 'swift-footed' even when he is sitting down to enjoy a feast, Hector always 'tamer of horses' even when, on foot, he is saying farewell to his beloved wife Andromache and letting his little son play with his helmet) must at all costs be avoided, if only because Pope in this translation, his major work, must display his own qualities, and essentially these were variety and a gift for the swift modulation of tone. So, all through, it might be said, as we sometimes say of an actor, Pope 'plays against the text'. Homer's card is formulaic repetition; Pope's is elegant variation. Homer is flat and bald, Pope allusive and ornate. It is in these translations that we find that unaccustomed avoidance of the plain word for the plain thing that has been called Pope's 'poetic diction'; it is not in fact *his* diction, but his piquant sauce for serving up Homer.

Thus, Mr Peter Quennell, in his excellent biography of Pope up to 1728, quotes a lovely line about the death of a gallant squire, Clytus, slain by Teucer's 'thrilling arrow':

In youth's first bloom reluctantly he dies . . .

The elegiac pathos of the line is, Mr Quennell acutely points out, largely due to the beautiful choice and pacing of the adverb 'reluctantly'. But Mr Quennell adds: 'We owe [this] to the translator's unaided fancy: Homer's hero is described neither as reluctant to leave the world, nor, indeed, as very young.' Dr Johnson, a much deeper classical scholar than Pope, felt this sort of licence not only defensible but necessary; the English reader, he told Boswell, would find a bald and literal version of Homer absolutely unreadable. Johnson was probably right in that, if they are honest, modern readers find the exact hexameter version of Homer by the American scholar and poet, Professor Richmond Lattimore (generally acknowledged as the best modern version) less pleasurable reading than Pope. To reverse Bentley's polite sneer, which Pope never forgave: "You must not call it Homer, Mr Pope; but 'tis a pretty poem."

Before we get down to detailed criticism, let us remind ourselves of how Homer touches Pope's personal history. In 1715, Addison's cautious indication of preference for Tickell's version of the first book of the *Iliad*, as against Pope's version (a trial of public approval) of the first four books, crystallised Pope's dislike of Addison's manner, certainly unjustified towards a genius like Pope, of polite condescension. And, much later, there was a great deal of discussion of how generous, or how mean, Pope was with his two collaborators in the *Odyssey*, Fenton and Broome. Pope translated the *Iliad* on his own, and was exhausted at the end of the successful effort; but he 'undertook a translation' of the *Odyssey* with the aid of two minor poets but better Greek scholars than himself, Broome and Fenton. He translated twelve of the twenty-four books of the *Odyssey* himself, Broome eight, Fenton four. Pope, however, polished their work. In his own *Iliad*, the polishing was his real pleasure; he aimed at first at about forty lines a day, using the Dacier French version and Chapman's earlier English version as well as Homer himself and Latin notes and commentaries on him. He would make three or four drafts, designed to get the sense clear, and then thrust his books aside and work on his own verse, aiming at making it as elegant and expressive as possible. Apart from this final polishing, the rest of the work, which kept him hours a day at his writing table, must have been painful and obstinate drudgery. His polishing of the Broome and Fenton books may have made all the difference between plodding and poetry; outside the *Odyssey*, neither made any memorable contribution to English verse. Certainly, neither Broome nor Fenton felt that he was fairly treated but they were thinking of the way Pope kept his name in the foreground and theirs in the background. Neither complained that he was mean about money. He may, however, have been thinking of the profits of the book in keeping them in the background. The *Iliad* had been a very great financial success; the *Odyssey* at first sold comparatively slowly and it was prudent of Pope to increase its popularity by emphasising his own major share in the work.

A side of Pope's character that saddens one is shown less, perhaps, in his treatment of Broome and Fenton than in his posthumous treatment of Addison, arising originally from the coolness about Tickell, and Pope's sense that Addison was pushing Tickell's version against his. He deliberately left his elegant and genuinely admiring epistle to Addison, on the latter's *Dialogue on Medals*, out of the 1717 volume. It made its appearance instead as a prefatory poem, very ironically to Tickell's own edition of Addison's *Works*, which appeared in 1721, two years after Addison's death. Pope would get every credit for magnanimity, and the dead Addison no pleasure, out of this posthumous compliment. But earlier on, in Addison's lifetime, Pope had sent the essayist that famous character of Addison which, very many years after Addison's death, was to become the most coolly balanced piece of satire (as the Sporus passage is the most hysterical) in the *Epistle to Dr Arbuthnot*. Addison, after receiving the first draft, as Pope complacently remarked, 'used me very civilly ever after'; it was clearly extremely dangerous *not* to use Mr Pope very civilly. One may, however, be rather appalled at the appearance of the Atticus passage so late as the *Epistle to Dr Arbuthnot*. The two excuses are that it is too splendid a piece of writing to have been wasted, and that it is in a sense impersonal satire, on a permanent type, the successful but not great writer who likes to be surrounded by flatterers, and who distrusts rising genius, rather than a mere revenge on Addison. Nevertheless, what Cardinal Manning with a sighing chuckle said of Cardinal Newman is true of Pope: 'He was a good hater!'

It is pleasanter to turn to the virtues of the translations. In Pope's prefaces with their vivid insistence that 'Homer is universally allow'd to have had the greatest Invention of any Writer whatever', there is an agreeable unfeigned enthusiasm. Homer for Pope is clearly the fount of all secular, as the Bible is the fount of all sacred, literature. He is not to be spoken of without a kind of awe. Virgil may equal Homer in judgment but no writer at all equals him in natural power. After all, all that Art as distinct from Nature (and to the poet Homer and Nature are identical ideas) can do is 'as in the most regular Gardens . . . reduce the beauties of Nature to more regularity, and such a Figure, which the common Eye may better take in, and is therefore more entertain'd with'. Pope was writing at a time when the irregular garden, of which the most beautiful example in England is still perhaps Stourhead, designed by Kent, was coming in. Round the artificial lake are temples and a grotto in which, beside a water nymph, is an inscription from Pope. Wherever one stops on the circuit round the lake one is faced with a subtly different vista. Kent was the earliest, the most intimate, perhaps the most romantic of all the great landscape gardeners of the eighteenth century. To the complimentary, but half-ironical question, in a poem by one of the Wartons, 'Can Kent design like Nature?' the answer is perhaps 'Almost!' One should visit Stourhead, appreciate these temples, these changing vistas, this artifice of wildness, before embarking on Pope's Homer. The house at Stourhead, incidentally, is designed in the Palladian style, invented by Palladio for Venetian noblemen in Vicenza, and based on the theory that the beauty of Nature is the beauty of mathematical proportion. We shall see what Pope is aiming at in his Homer if we contrast the garden and the house, and think of Pope as aiming at a kind of harmony and contrast between an underlying principle of order and its bewildering and rich expression in life. Pope himself puts it neatly:

> the reason why most Critics are inclin'd to prefer a judicious and methodical Genius to a great and fruitful one, is, because they find it easier for themselves to pursue their Observations through an uniform and bounded Walk of Art, than to comprehend the vast and various Extent of Nature.

This frank contempt for 'most critics' and their wish to keep poetry tidy is in splendid contradiction to, at least, yesterday's or the day before yesterday's received ideas about Pope.

The great task was also a kind of martyrdom. Homer was to eat up ten years, a little more or less, of Pope's life. He assured himself fame and financial independence for the rest of his life; more importantly, perhaps, for his inner self, the sense that his liking for 'the great' depended on no need of their patronage and that he could receive and return their hospitality as an equal. But there were sleepless nights; nightmares of an endless journey, in which a point was reached in great weariness, and then another journey just as long stretched ahead. When the long task ended with the publication of the last two volumes of the *Odyssey* in 1726, Pope was in his late thirties. Many of his friends were away from him (Swift was in Ireland, and though Bolingbroke was back in England, this was not till 1725, and he was fairly soon, under

Walpole's threats, to depart again). Pope was ill and prematurely old. Yet he had created a masterpiece from which great writers as different as Gibbon and Ruskin learned their first idea of Homer. Even Arnold, who so disliked Pope and all the chilling breezes of the eighteenth century, admitted that of all Homer's English translations only Pope's captured Homer's swiftness. If we consider Pope's Homer as an original work (and there is some reason for doing so) he will rank among the half-dozen or so post-Renaissance poets (I leave more recent and dubiously established poems from the Browning of *The Ring and the Book*, through Doughty and Hardy's *Dynasts* to Pound's *Cantos* aside) who have written classic long poems in our language; the Spenser of the *Faerie Queen*, the Milton of *Paradise Lost*, the Dryden of the English version of the *Aeneid*, the Wordsworth of *The Prelude* (and my colleague, Isobel Armstrong, would add of *The Excursion*) and the Byron of *Don Juan*.

But the strain must have been nearly unbearable. Pope, was, by inclination, above all a poet of personal feeling; between 1717 and 1726 he wrote only one of the first order, the noble *Epistle to Oxford* prefaced to the posthumous works of the genial but intemperate Irish poet and clergyman Thomas Parnell (an ancestor of Charles Stewart Parnell) who had died young partly of grief for the death of his wife:

Such were the notes thy once-lov'd Poet sung,
'Till Death untimely stop'd his tuneful Tongue . . .

The poem praises Harley for his courage in the tower and his stoicism when he had retreated to his country estates. Harley, the honest but muddled politician, felt he had hardly the Roman virtues ascribed to him by Pope, but deprived of power for ever and in declining health, was all the more touched by the poem. If Pope never forgave an enemy, he never deserted a fallen friend.

But let us look at Homer itself. One passage of Homer with which many modern readers are acquainted is the raising of ghosts from a pit into which the blood of sacrificial animals has been shed, after Odysseus and his companions have fled from Circe's isle. The first ghost they see is that of their drunken companion Elpenor, who had broken his neck falling down a ladder of Circe's palace, and for whom the hurry of the occasion had not allowed them to perform any burial rites. People know this passage because it is at the centre of Pound's first *Canto*, translated not direct from Homer but from a Renaissance Latin version of Homer which Pound had picked up from a second-hand bookstall in Italy; and translated not in the manner of Homer or in a Renaissance Latin style but in the Old English style which Pound had learned by translating (vividly and powerfully, though at moments very obscurely or inaccurately) the melancholy monologue *The Seafarer*. There are, in a way, as many layers of language between Pound and Homer as between Pope and Homer. But Pound, of course, unlike Pope, feels 'modern':

> But first Elpenor came, our friend Elpenor,
> Unburied, cast on the wide earth,
> Limbs that we left in the house of Circe,
> Unwept, unwrapped in sepulchre, since toils urged other,
> Pitiful spirit. And I cried in hurried speech:
> 'Elpenor, how art thou come to this dark coast?
> 'Cam'st thou afoot, outstripping seamen?'
>   And he in heavy speech:
> 'Ill fate and abundant wine. I slept in Circe's ingle.
> Going down the long ladder unguarded,
> I fell against the buttress,
> Shattered the nape-nerve, the soul sought Avernus.
> 'But thou, O King, I bid remember me, unwept, unburied,
> 'Heap up mine arms, be tomb by sea-bord, and inscribed:
> '*A man of no fortune, and with a name to come.*
> 'And set my oar up, that I swung mid fellows.'

Admirers of Pound, even those who think that the *Cantos* as a whole are a failure, would judge this to be one of the great passages of modern poetry; as a teacher, I have found that its pathos, swiftness, immediacy, and simplicity work on students who do not know the Homeric story, and are frankly incurious about it. Let us see how Pope deals with the same source. The passage is at line 65 of Pope's version of Book XI of the *Odyssey* (one of the books he did entirely by himself, with no help from Broome or Fenton):

> There, wand'ring thro' the gloom I first survey'd,
> New to the realms of death, *Elpenor's* shade:
> His cold remains all naked to the sky
> On distant shores unwept, unburied lye.
> Sad at the sight I stand, deep fix'd in woe,
> And ere I spoke the tears began to flow.
>   O say what angry pow'r *Elpenor* led
> To glide in shades, and wander with the dead?

How could thy soul, by realms and seas disjoyn'd,
Out fly the nimble sail, and leave the lagging wind?
  The Ghost reply'd: To Hell my doom I owe,
Daemons accurst, dire ministers of woe!
My feet thro' wine unfaithful to their weight,
Betray'd me tumbling from a tow'ry height,
Stagg'ring I reel'd, and as I reel'd I fell,
Lux'd the neck joynt – my soul descends to hell.
But lend me aid, I now conjure thee lend,
By the soft tye and sacred name of friend!
By thy fond consort! by thy father's cares!
By lov'd *Telemachus* his blooming years!
For well I know that soon the heav'nly pow'rs
Will give thee back to day, and *Circe's* shores:
There pious on my cold remains attend,
There call to mind thy poor departed friend.
The tribute of a tear is all I crave,
And the possession of a peaceful grave.
But if unheard, in vain compassion plead,
Revere the Gods, the Gods avenge the dead!
A tomb along the wat'ry margin raise,
The tomb with manly arms and trophies grace,
To show posterity *Elpenor* was.
There high in air, memorial of my name,
Fix the smooth oar, and bid me live to fame.

This passage is longer than Pound's but, rather than blaming Pope
for redundancies, we should note that Pound is drastic in omissions.
Here from a modern American translation by Professor Ennis Rees
(New York, 1960) is the passage which Pope paraphrases and Pound
leaves out. (One should note that Rees, writing in accentual hexameters.
though neither accentual nor quantitative hexameters lend themselves
easily to English, is closer than either Pope or Pound to Homer's
rhythms, but he attempts, unlike the other two, a quite literal, word
by word, reproduction of Homer's sense):

  'Now I have something to ask in the name
Of those at home, your wife and your father that raised you
And your only son Telemachus, for I'm sure that after
You leave this kingdom you'll stop for a while at that
Aegean island with your excellent ship. . .'

And then Rees continues at the point where Pound picks up again:
                                                              'There,
O King, I beg you, remember me. Do not
Leave me behind unwept and unburied, for then
You'll surely have me to haunt you . . .'

Pound leaves out the threat of haunting which Pope renders peri-
phrastically:

But if unheard, in vain compassion plead,
Revere the Gods, the Gods avenge the dead!

Probably Pound felt that Elpenor's plight should arouse in us a single
concentrated emotion, compassion, and that if Elpenor, with a hint of
blackmail, begins to threaten the heroic Odysseus he will also arouse
dislike. Pope, again with Odysseus's dignity in mind, felt that the
threat had to be very indirect (with the stress on the anger of the Gods
rather than on the wrath of Elpenor's ghost, the ghost of a somewhat
contemptible character). Before leaving Professor Rees's version,
obviously the most useful of all three as a crib to Homer, one had
regretfully to admit that it is not very exciting, and seems to bear out
Johnson's suggestion that a literal version of Homer would be unattrac-
tive. The other two, at least, read like poetry; sadly and ironically,
the literal version does not.

Pope's very interesting footnotes on this passage show that he was
puzzled both by the *point* of the Elpenor passage at this point in the
narrative and by a crux in verbal translation, the proper rendering of
the line which Pound gives (correctly) as 'Cam'st thou afoot, out-
stripping seamen?':

73.   How could thy soul, by realms and seas disjoyn'd,
         Out-fly the nimble sail?

Eustathius is of opinion, that *Ulysses* speaks pleasantly [*modern
meaning, wittily, jokingly,* GSF] to *Elpenor*, for were his words to
be literally translated they would be, *Elpenor, thou art come hither
on foot, sooner than I in a ship*. I suppose it is the worthless character
of *Elpenor* that led that Critic into this opinion; but I would rather
take the sentence to be spoken seriously, not only because such
railleries are an insult upon the unfortunate, and levities perhaps
unworthy of Epic Poetry, but also from the general conduct of
Ulysses, who at the sight of *Elpenor* bursts into tears, and com-

passionates the fate of his friend. Is there any thing in this that looks like raillery? if there be, we must confess that *Ulysses* makes a very quick translation from sorrow to pleasantry.

Such quick translations (or, as we would say now, transitions) are, however, very common in great poetry and admirably illustrate Freud's theory of the joke as a safety-valve through which extremely painful emotions are given a harmless and even superficially pleasurable outlet. They may be also a way of expressing sympathy of a deep kind, that does not want to express itself sentimentally. Shakespeare's Hamlet often speaks 'pleasantly' in this way – his 'Very like, very like!' when told that the spectacle of the ghost would have much astonished him – and his 'madness' can be taken as a way of making an inner turmoil bearable by turning it into bitter jests. Donne's famous stanza at the beginning of 'A Feaver' is another example of 'speaking pleasantly', at once masking and expressing more pungently a sense of extreme agony:

> Oh doe not die, for I shall hate
> All women so, when thou art gone,
> That thee I shall not celebrate,
> When I remember thou wast one.

It does suggest some kind of limitation in the Augustan sensibility that Pope, unlike Homer himself, unlike Shakespeare, Donne, or Pound, cannot respond to this special fusion of grief and wit, this 'trench-humour' as the soldiers of the First World War called it.

Pope takes the whole story very seriously and works painstakingly at its logic. He notes that Odysseus has raised Tiresias, the blind prophet, from Hades but that Elpenor is the first ghost he sees moving; Elpenor moves so rapidly because unlike the other raised ghosts he is not rising gloomily out of Hades but hurrying with horror down into it. And yet has Elpenor enough dignity to be the first ghost to be described in detail? Pope's answer to this question shows up a certain priggishness in Augustan thinking. It might be Addison himself speaking:

> But it may be ask'd what connection this story of *Elpenor* has to the subject of the Poem, and what it contributes to the end of it? *Bossu* very well answers that the Poet may insert some incidents that make no part of the fable or action; especially if they be short, and break not the thread of it: this before us is only a small part of a

large episode, which the Poet was at liberty to insert or omit, as contributed most to the beauty of his poetry; besides, it contains an excellent moral, and shews us the ill effects of drunkenness and debauchery. The Poet represents *Elpenor* as a person of a mean character, and punishes his crime with sudden death, and dishonour.

But Bossu's answer, and Pope's endorsement of it, will not do. The effect of the episode of *Elpenor's* ghost, with its homeliness and pathos, its almost tragic absurdity, at the beginning of Book XI, is to set us down in the real human world of sympathetic weakness and thus make us readier to accept the growingly remote and awesome phantasms that, in Homer's pageant from Hades, succeed Elpenor. The Elpenor episode has something to the effect which De Quincey attributed to the soliloquy of the drunken porter and the knocking on the gate in *Macbeth*: the sense of a real world, a 'mean' world if Pope likes to put it so, holding our half-comic, half-pitying attention, and when the gate is opened, when the porter or Elpenor is swept off stage, revealing horror.

Elpenor is our bridge, in the very weaknesses we share with him, in his lack of obvious heroic qualities, between this world and the next. He is no hero, his death was absurd and ridiculous (perhaps he was climbing down the ladder to find a place to empty his bladder of 'abundant wine'). But Odysseus responds most sympathetically – which is to say that Homer responds to human weakness as generously as Shakespeare – to Elpenor's request to be given the sort of tomb he would have had *if* he had been a hero. After all, it was bloody bad luck ('ill fate') that Elpenor died in such a humiliating way and never had the chance (*'A man of no fortune, and with a name to come'*) to show the stuff that was in him. Most great poets, at most other times, would have had the generosity of imagination to see this. This generosity Pope and his age did not quite possess; and it is for this reason that Arnold's question about whether Augustan poetry is poetry in the highest sense can never be quite finally dismissed.

Let us look, however, at this text of Pope's with an alert eye for those positive qualities in it that are delightful. Let us notice first one place in which Pope, Pound, and Rees almost completely coincide: Pound and Pope have 'unwept, unburied' and Rees 'unwept and unburied'. Perhaps they are simply the most apt and original words for the sense of the original. A good translator (in their different ways Pope, Pound, and the scholarly Rees are all translators) will never be afraid of the version which is at once most obvious and most apt. But now let us look, rather, at the originalities of Pope. Pope's central fear is that because of the character of Elpenor this may appear a 'low' passage. He seeks to avoid that impression by aiming at intense pathos, expressed through musicality:

> His cold remains all naked to the sky
> On distant shores unwept, unburied lye.
> Sad at the sight I stand, deep fix'd in woe,
> And ere I spoke the tears began to flow.

Note the repeated use of l's, r's, d's, liquids and unvoiced dentals and of alliterative sibilants – 'Sad at the sight I stand.' Notice, also, the long open diphthongs for rhymes, 'sky', 'lye', 'woe', 'flow'. The consonants within the line sometimes clench the feeling, sometimes let it trickle forward, but the grief opens out like a great sigh at the rhyming words. Such smoothness, however, could become monotonous for 'oft the ear the open vowels tire' and therefore suddenly we get an expressive rather than euphonious line, a little irregularly scanned, whose movement suggests the tacking and bobbing of a small boat between veering winds:

> Out-fly the nimble sail, and leave the lagging wind? . . .

But then Elpenor has to die, drunk, missing his step on a ladder, and breaking his neck. How is Pope going to manage this with dignity? Neither Pope nor ourselves nor perhaps Homer, using raw material transmitted orally to him perhaps over four centuries, can be sure about the architecture and sleeping arrangements of Circe's palace. 'Ingle' means fire or hearth and if, as in Pound's version, you have to climb down a long ladder from an ingle, why? A hearth is on the ground floor. And if you were 'in the ingle' (accepting the word, rather reluctantly, as metonymy for 'house') how, again as in Pound, could you strike your neck 'against the Buttress', a supportive feature jutting from *outside* the house? Taking my picture from Pound I put Elpenor in an attic with a perpendicular wooden ladder descending from it to the great hall, but he would then go smash on the floor beneath him, not on a buttress. Rees makes it clearer but not utterly clear:

> When I woke up in the house
> Of Circe, I did not remember that long ladder
> By which I came up and proceeded to fall headlong
> From the roof, fatally breaking my neck.

For Rees, how did he get up to the roof from 'in the house' except by a ladder, and was there another ladder leading down from the flat roof to the grounds? (What I find myself broadly imagining is a great hall with an alcove in the corner for Circe's couch, where she and Odysseus would sleep. After their evening feast, Odysseus's companions would climb up a ladder to a kind of attic, but the ladder would continue to a flat roof, where they might prefer to sleep on mild spring and summer nights. There would almost certainly be a ladder leading up to this roof from outside, as well as the ladder leading up to the attic from the hall.) Perhaps Pope's very vagueness is tactful here and Elpenor's memories of the geography of the house were still, even in his ghostly state, drunken and confused:

> My feet thro' wine unfaithful to their weight,
> Betray'd me tumbling from a tow'ry height,
> Staggring I reel'd, and as I reel'd I fell,
> Lux'd the neck joynt – my soul descends to hell.

Lux'd' was a shorter form of the technical medical term to 'luxate' or 'dislocate'. It is first recorded in 1708, where it is used in John Philips's very popular mock-heroic poem *Cyder*: Philips is clearly Pope's source for 'lux'd' and the equally technical 'neck joynt': for they both come from a passage in *Cyder* where he makes fun of the Elpenor story:

> What shall we say
> Of rash *Elpenor*, who in evil hour
> Dry'd an immeasurable Bowl, and thought
> T'exhale his Surfeit by Irriguous Sleep,
> Imprudent? Him, Death's Iron-Sleep opprest,
> Descending careless from his Couch; the Fall
> Luxt his Neck-joint, and spinal Marrow bruised.

It is interesting that what Philips seems to have in mind is bunks in tiers as in a barracks or second-class sleeping car with ladders down from the top couch. For him, Elpenor's fall is quite a short one but sufficient not only to dislocate his neck but to bruise his spine. For Pope, no doubt, the new form 'lux'd' had the appeal of having the precision but not the air of technical pedantry (something he always avoided) of the old 'luxated'. Pope does what he can for the dignity of Elpenor's feet 'thro' wine unfaithful to their weight' and his deliberately vague 'tow'ry height' is emotionally impressive and slips gently round the question of where exactly Elpenor was when he fell, and where he fell to. He dodges, also, the problems raised by the ladder, an undignified piece of furniture by neo-classic standards of the high style. But the couplet in which Elpenor's fall is made real to us is, as mimetic verse, a triumph: in two lines, we are dizzy, we are slipping, fall, break our necks – hell opens for us. Whatever other non-Popian virtues Pound's version may have, Pound could never have equalled the sheer speed of this:

Stagg'ring I reel'd, and as I reel'd I fell,
Lux'd the neck joynt – my soul descends to hell.

The rest of the passage aims at pathos and dignity and achieves these at the cost of depriving Elpenor of that bitter individuality he has in Homer and retains in Pound. The ghost seems at the end to be any dead person at all of high rank, his rank defined by the nobility of his pleading voice:

There high in air, memorial of my name,
Fix the smooth oar, and bid me live to fame.
    To whom with tears: These rites, on mournful shade,
Due to thy Ghost, shall to thy Ghost be paid.

For all the tears, and the use of the word 'mournful', Pope's Ulysses seems oddly brisk here, very much the colonel getting rid of the awkward sub-lieutenant: 'Request granted, Elpenor: Elpenor, dismiss!' This may reflect Pope's discomfort, shown in his notes, with the whole passage. Whether deliberate or not, a certain polite irony in the last line reflects the same discomfort:

These rites . . .
Due to thy Ghost, shall to thy Ghost be paid.

The rites, one cannot help reflecting, were hardly due to anything Elpenor had achieved, not as a ghost, but as a man.

Pound and Pope are both great poets (Pound is at his best rather less frequently than Pope but, when he is at his best, is the master of devices of verse and ranges of feeling more complex than Pope's age imagined). But, examining this particular passage, one decides that Pope is much more concrete than he at first seems, Pound much less. Pound's ladder and buttress and ingle are like wooden bricks which a child cannot pile on each other to make a real house. Pope, especially when dealing with motion, when quietly but terrifyingly speeding things up – uncertain feet, a slip, a fall, a broken neck, hell – gives a sense of supple and real and changing *movement* under his verbal elegances. Pope's is a concreteness of motion – and of emotion – rather than of physical object. But too much of Homer in the style of Ezra Pound's Elpenor passage would be static: Pound's style suits the isolation, turning almost into still life, of a high moment in a rapidly moving poem. Pope's style and his Augustan sense of the shape and drive of Homer as a whole lend themselves admirably to the changes of pace and tone needed in great narrative poetry. He understood, as Pound, with his brilliant and early exploitation of Imagism, and his fascination with Vorticism and Cubism, perhaps never did, that readers of a long poem are interested in actions and people set in a narrative continuity, more than in fragmentary and isolated documentations, and certainly more than in things. It is Pound's weakness that in the *Cantos* he gives us no coherent picture of the motives or fate of one of his Renaissance heroes, Malatesta who built the Tempio at Rimini, and on the other hand enchants us, lyrically, in an early *Canto*, with a picture of the sea-nymphs, the colour of the Mediterranean, olive-trees and the light on them, which has no narrative interest at all. As a translator, Pope was lucky to be a master of euphony and expressiveness within a limited verse-scheme, but not primarily a lyric poet. Anybody today who tackles his Homer will to his surprise find himself reading one of the few English long poems which is easily readable; a vivid story with characters who are actual people. And, as Mr H. A. Mason has pointed out, Pope in his own spirit and genius is not so utterly unlike Homer that he cannot help us when we attempt to master Homer himself.

5

An Essay on Man: Pope as a Poet of Cosmic Order

Pope's fiercest satire and the poem that made him not only admired but feared and formidable, *The Dunciad*, came out in 1728, but it was intermittently altered and added to to the end of his life, and I shall defer its consideration to the fourth section of this critical anatomy, when I consider Pope as a satirist (often as a much more good-natured and tolerant satirist than *The Dunciad* suggests he was), and deal here with Pope as a philosophical poet, a poet concerned with the grounds of religion in *An Essay on Man* (published anonymously, first three epistles 1733, fourth epistle 1734) and the *Moral Essays*, sometimes called *Epistles to Several Persons* (Mr F. W. Bateson's Twickenham title), of which the first, the *Epistle to Burlington*, came out in 1731, those to Bathurst and Cobham in 1733 and 1734, and the delightful and lively *Of The Characters of Women* (addressed, but not by name, to Martha Blount) in 1735.

These poems are part of a larger scheme that was never completed and the ideas in them cohere. Pope's God is above our understanding, our happiness is certainly not his sole purpose but we must believe it is one of his purposes. To activate us, he has given us all self-love and a ruling passion; but if we are humble and obedient to him we find that self-love, the quest for happiness, fulfils itself best when it transforms itself into social love. To be good is to be happy. Some ruling passions, like patriotism and benevolence, are direct roads to virtue. Others, like vanity and affectation, are silly if not positively wicked and men should be gently laughed out of them. Others *are* wicked and should, if they cannot be punished, at least be publicly denounced, so that the bad can perhaps be shamed into the pretence of virtue. Pope had no doubt that happiness is the proper end at which all men should aim, that the happiness of the universe as a whole is what God aims at, which is why we should worship and obey Him without attempting to probe his higher and more mysterious purposes, that we shall be best fitted to obey him if we try to study our own characters and motives intelligently, and that such a study will in the end teach us that the truest happiness is to be found in widespread social sympathy and active benevolence. Thus a clear-sighted pursuit of virtue leads to happiness, but a clear-sighted pursuit of happiness also leads to virtue.

Though Pope had read Fénelon and Pascal, and though he was unswervingly loyal to the Roman Catholic Church, when he sets out in *An Essay on Man* to 'vindicate the ways of God to man', he is defending the all-powerful, wholly just, and transcendent God of any monotheistic religion. Very widely translated, *An Essay on Man* appealed to cultivated Muslims as well as Christians, and Bolingbroke, who suggested to Pope many of the arguments in the poem, was a Deist. Pope realised that the Christian mysteries as such were beyond the scope of such an argument. But there is nothing in the poem to offend Christians (the Swiss Professor, Crousaz, who attacked *An Essay on Man*, was both working with an inaccurate translation and was a fanatical Calvinist) unless, like Karl Barth, they object to any attempt to produce arguments for the existence of a God and of that God's goodness, and demand instead unquestioning submission to Holy Writ. Pope's standpoint was humbler. At the Court of James II, one of James's chaplains, attempting to convert to Roman Catholicism a powerful but libertine Lord, said: 'You will allow, my Lord, the existence of a Supreme Being . . .' The nobleman turned on the priest coldly: 'Why should you suppose so?' To allow the existence of a Supreme Being and to produce arguments for submission to him may, at least, lay the foundation for that higher spiritual life, that awareness of the *mysterium tremendum*, to which Pope was both too formal in his religious adherence – his Roman Catholicism, if not his Christianity, was largely a matter of devotion to his parents and affection for early rescusant friends like Caryll and the Blounts – and too genuinely aware of his own spiritual limitations to aspire. He felt quite certain at least about happiness as an ultimate aim, about social virtue and benevolence as means to it, and about submission to God as the beginning of virtue.

The best introduction to *An Essay on Man* is Professor Maynard Mack's introduction to the Twickenham Edition, and particularly its conclusion. Professor Mack deals very thoroughly with the sources of the poem. These are in the main – in spite of the claims made for Bolingbroke – those sources available to any writer in the Western tradition from the late Stoics and neo-Platonists through the Christian fathers to writers nearer Pope's own time, like Spinoza, or roughly contemporary with him, like Leibniz. Pope was writing a theodicy. A theodicy takes it for granted that there is a God, at once powerful and benevolent. Why did this God create a world in which there is so much pain and sin, and so much that falls short of perfection, even in its own limited kind?

Part of the answer is that, according to at least the vast majority of moral theologians, even God's omnipotence has its limits in what, without disrespect to God, we can call 'the nature of things'. God, for instance – though this is not a point that comes into Pope's poem – cannot will the past to have been other than it was. He cannot will the same proposition, say that Great Britain is an island, to be simultaneously both true and untrue, and he cannot even will such an apparently trivial thing as that a visually sensible object should be coloured without being extended. As the sole perfect being in the universe, God cannot create another being of a perfection equal to his own. Why then should God, being perfect, and perfectly happy in Himself, create anything at all?

Traditional theology sees the creation of the universe as an act of generosity in which God extends his love into a free chain of created beings; the nine orders of archangels and angels, who are wholly spiritual and who have intuitive and immediate knowledge (they do not require to practise the laborious process of reasoning); man, who is partly spiritual and partly a rational animal, who has intuitive knowledge of some things (like the difference between right and wrong), but mostly works things out through reasoning from experience, and sometimes with a biased reason, for he has a body, passions, and senses, and passions and senses may lead him wilfully or blindly to deceive himself; man is given power over the animals, but depends on them largely for food, clothing, and locomotion, as they in their turn depend on his care; animals, unlike man, have no reason, no fear of death, but like man have instincts and feelings; the vegetable creation has life, and provides man with wholesome food and the enjoyment of natural beauty, but unlike man and animals neither enjoys nor suffers; the geological universe has not even the minimal life of the plants, but it provides the stage on which the human drama is acted. There is thus a hierarchy, a great chain of being, and at each link of this chain God has provided each kind of creature with the sort of perfection it deserves or needs. Since God works by general laws, there must be some sin and some suffering, though these must serve purposes which are divine but beyond the capacity of man's understanding.

Reason itself, for Pope, and for the tradition of thought he is working in, is not a motive, and so man needs passions to spur him into action. These passions can spur men into the vices of a Borgia or a Catiline as well as the virtues of a Decius or a Curtius. Just so, the same general laws that produce a trade wind will occasionally produce an earthquake. God uses wickedness and disaster in the end to increase goodness. Maynard Mack quotes a passage from St Augustine, which I translate more literally than he:

> Just as bad men make a bad use of created things that are good . . .
> so the Creator makes a good use of bad men . . . The painter
> knows where to put his black coloration so that the picture is
> properly effective; and shall God not know where to put the
> sinner so that the sinner may be among the created things ordained
> to a good use?

It is up to man therefore, Pope feels (but he is saying something very traditional, not something startlingly new) to accept God's purposes and to accept, which may be more difficult, his own limited power to understand them; in man's case, as in that of God's other creatures, he knows as much as is good for him. The more man submits to God's purposes and instead of striving rebelliously after the condition of the angels thinks instead of the condition of the animals, creatures whom he makes use of but also feeds, shelters, and protects, the more man will see that the apparent contradictions of this world are resolved in a higher harmony. Submitting to God's decrees, man will see that self-love finds its true fulfilment in social love and that even our strongest ruling passions, when scrutinised ('The proper study of Mankind is Man') and checked by our reason, lead us to find the truest happiness in contentment with our own state and benevolence towards the state of others.

An Essay on Man, translated and acclaimed in both Protestant and Catholic countries, was (leaving the translation of Homer aside) the greatest critical success in his lifetime of all Pope's original poems. Various complaints have been made against it; Dr Johnson felt that its arguments were shallow and familiar, and that Pope was out of his intellectual depth. It has been said that there is nothing new in it, that it does not solve the problem of evil (who has?), that its arguments would give no comfort at all if one were suffering from acute pain in a hospital. They might comfort one, Maynard Mack points out, when one was reflecting on one's recent sufferings in convalescence. As argument, of course, the weakest part of Pope's, as of any, theodicy is the leap from the general argument that this world is as perfect as God can make it – Pope agreed with Bolingbroke that it is wishful thinking to argue from injustices and imperfections in this world to the existence of a next world created specifically to redress these – to the ethical part of the argument that we are all in great danger of being led by our ruling passions into folly or vice, though also in some hopes of being spurred by these passions into virtue. In one sense (I paraphrase and summarise Maynard Mack's line of argument) we are perfectly at home in this world, it is the place of our bustle, our useful activities, our enjoyable self-importance. In another sense, we know that we do not belong to the bustle, we are spectators rather than actors, we watch our own show of self-importance with rueful irony:

I, a stranger and afraid,
In a world I never made . . .

Most men share, or alternate, Housman's sad alienation with Pope's cheerful involvement. That Pope did not see the Housman side limits, in a way, the claims to greatness of *An Essay on Man*.

Maynard Mack, who does see *An Essay on Man* as a poem at least of some greatness, does not claim that it is a masterpiece of reasoning in verse, like Dryden's *Religio Laici*. But it recreates the feelings connected with the reasoning which Dryden presents, almost stripped of feeling, in its strong, bare dryness. The lack of logical coherence in *An Essay on Man* may account for its appeal to a wide range of human sympathies. True, Pope was no philosopher, he was versifying (very vulnerable) ideas which a true scholar, like Dr Johnson, felt he had often met before. Mack defends the incoherence, or the weakness of the links in the glittering chain of aphorisms, thus:

Popular thought on many subjects . . . is often less significant for
coherence than for keeping alive, together, conflicting but valuable
points of view . . . that motive is the right standard of human
virtue – but so is result; that man's affective nature is inferior to
the best that is in him – but it is a contributory cause of what is
best; that man is pitiable or contemptible when looked at in
himself – yet somehow strong and good when looked at with
reference to his potentialities. If, as Hulme says, the starting point
of religious attitudes is always the kind of subject found in Pascal,

69

the vanity of desire, their ending point is always in the value of some aspect of the agent in whom the vain desires take place: *misère*, but not without *grandeur*.

Pascal belonged, of course, to the generation before Pope's. But he is like Pope in his combination of lifelong invalidism and pain with polished courtly manners (manners, like Pope's, above his station by birth), with mastery of style, indefatigable industry, and a cruelly piercing and deeply serious wit. He felt like Pope the attractions of the great world and the ruling passion that was the great temptation of both men was a defiant pride. 'However strong one may be,' Pascal notes, 'it may happen that one feels the need to submit oneself to somebody or something; the least humiliating course is always to submit oneself to God.' 'Life', Pascal also wrote, 'is a slightly less inconsistent dream': and one thinks of the pretty dream of *The Rape of the Lock*, the choking nightmare of *The Dunciad*. To Louis Racine, who attacked *An Essay on Man* in 1742 on the strength of a very inaccurate translation by du Resnel, Pope wrote, with the politeness he would always show to a fellow Roman Catholic, that his thoughts about natural religion far from being 'those of Spinoza, or even of Leibniz' were 'on the contrary conformable to those of Mons. Pascal & Mons. Fénelon: the latter of whom I would most readily imitate in submitting all my Opinions to the Decision of the Church.'

One wishes one knew a little more about how deep Pope was in Pascal. A line like:

The glory, jest, and riddle of the world,

seems to lay more stress on the *grandeur* than on the *misère* of man: a jest can be glorious, and there is dignity and mystery in being a riddle. Pope was an Erasmian by temperament. In the great controversy of the previous century about necessary and sufficient grace, the resistible or irresistible strength of grace, the degree of corruptness and the ability to act with virtue when not strongly tempted of man's fallen nature, Pope's temperament would have led him to the Jesuits and their Molinist point of view rather than to the Jansenists whom Pascal, early on, a little to their embarrassment, supported. (It was embarrassing that Pascal, in the *Provincial Letters*, should make abstruse theological questions lively and amusing reading for the general public, since the Jansenists hated both the ostentatious play of unusual temperament and the worldly enjoyment of witty writing; certainly their own ponderous writings compensated amply for Pascal's brilliance.) Pope believed that a virtuous and happy life was hard but by no means impossible to pursue, and Pascal believed that, without special grace, it was impossible. Pascal hated this world; Pope, even at least intermittently in his darkest moods of pain and depression, enjoyed it. Yet in *Les Lettres Provinciales* he must have admired Pascal's destructive wit and ruthless honesty. Sentences in *Les Pensées* must have stuck in his mind.

Brilliant as Maynard Mack's introduction to *An Essay on Man* is (indeed, still the most perceptive and thorough study of the poem), it was written in 1947, nearer Pope's world than it is near even to the academic world of today. Mack saw Pope as turning abstractions into art; as celebrating a world of objective order by turning into a dance of concepts the sort of vindication or justification of the ways of God to Man – and the defence of Christian and classical virtue – that to Milton could still be imagined as myth and presented as epic. The abstractions were to become concrete again for Wordsworth, in *Tintern Abbey* and *The Prelude* but, to Mack, the cost of Wordsworth's clear sense of a divine 'presence' in nature is that

> Pope's objective reality is threatening to disappear entirely inward, to the point at which Coleridge will exclaim:
>
> O Lady! we receive but what we give,
> And in our life alone does Nature live . . .

Coleridge's mood of dejection is not, however, for Mack the whole truth . . .

> 'Tintern Abbey' and *The Prelude* stand as monuments – not, I think, burial monuments – to one version of the Ciceronian sentiment that there is some kind of objective order beyond man, and that he who does not obey it abandons his better self. Pope's *Essay* is also such a monument.

Today a dejection like Coleridge's has been expressed in the plays and novels of Samuel Beckett, though under the mask of wry comedy. The sense of the 'objective order beyond man' has been expressed in late works by two great poets, T. S. Eliot's *Four Quartets* and Wallace Steven's *Notes Towards a Supreme Fiction*. What is odd about these two masterpieces when one compares them (bearing *An Essay on Man* in mind) is that what is utterly convincing in *Four Quartets* is the author's feeling for place, for the suddenly revived memory, for the blending of continuity with change and loss, for the poet's need constantly to renew and refresh his language; what are less convincing are the purely religious passages. Yet Eliot was a Christian. Stevens, as we see in his fine early poem *Sunday Morning*, had rejected Christianity for a hedonistic paganism, accepting death, delighting in the sensuality of mortal beauty, whose rites, if it had any, would be open-air feasts and dances celebrating the life-giving, transitory life-giving, glory of the sun. Stevens, therefore, writes as an atheist and in *Notes Towards a Supreme Fiction* in the place of the lost or relinquished God he sets up an equally impossible ideal, the final and completely inclusive and satisfactory poem (Gods, of course, are human fictions as poems are) which will never, of course, be written. Yet in Steven's working out of this purely aesthetic conception, his own contribution towards the idea of an 'objective order beyond man' – though this will only exist in so far as man lends himself to the task, vain by definition, of creating it – there seems to be more of a genuine religious feeling than in Eliot's dutiful and hollow borrowings from the great mystics. There is again perhaps a religious authenticity in Beckett to whom the rejected Irish biblical Protestantism of his youth is at least 'a myth I am familiar with'. A theodicy like Pope's is the central topic of Tom Stoppard's brilliant comedy *Jumpers*. He treats with a certain respect Professor George Moore's arguments, which are rather like Pope's argument, for a God who for Stoppard's generation has not had to be denied since He has never skirted the edge of possibility.

The contrast, in other words, between the period when Mack was writing and today is that now not even Christians, or those with a wistful feeling about Christianity, put much stress on vindicating the ways of God to man. Many authentic Christians are ready to admit that the word God is itself hopelessly ambiguous or equivocal. Professor Elizabeth Anscombe, in her introduction to Wittgenstein's *Tractatus Logico-Philosophicus*, points out that Wittgenstein incidentally (it is not one of his conscious purposes) refutes the Cartesian proof (derived ultimately from the Anselmian proof) of the existence of God from the concept of God. It is perfectly true that the Christian concept of God, like neo-Platonic concepts of the One, seem to imply that what the concept refers to, if it exists at all, has eternal necessary existence; which is why Nietzsche's famous 'God is dead' feels like a logical blunder. (Either He never was, or the concept of death, if He exists, does not apply to Him.) If there were such an object of thought that it corresponded in its reality to the Christian concept of God, that object would have to exist by necessity (it is part of its concept that it cannot help existing); but it remains an open question whether the object of thought corresponds to a real object or not.

Similarly Pope's concept of God, a God who has to express himself in plenitude, or in filling out all the ranks of possible creatures from the highest to the lowest, does imply cosmic harmony, but it is an open question whether Pope's concept of God applies to anything real. Pope's God, like St Augustine's, is an artist, and he uses his skill to give men at least a glimpse of a universe that is an object of delight and awe. Wittgenstein's universe in the *Tractatus* had a similar plenitude; it was everything that was the case, and it could not admit any gaps. But the conception of a logically self-consistent world gave Wittgenstein no feeling of cosmic harmony. What was mystical was not *how* the world existed (finding out its basic pattern was for Wittgenstein a joyless task, asserting no values) but *that* it existed. That was the source of the mystical, and about the mystical nothing could be said clearly, so nothing should be said at all.

Miss Anscombe suggests that once one has grasped the basic logical pattern of the *Tractatus Logico-Philosophicus* one can read it for aesthetic pleasure (as one reads, for instance, *An Essay on Man*). Pope is not the sort of poet one thinks of as mystical, but Maynard Mack uses that word of the ultimate effect of *An Essay on Man*; in spite of the title, Mack thinks the 'sublime' passages – the most lofty and thrilling passages – are about God and cosmic harmony. He instances this passage from towards the end of the fourth Epistle (lines 361 to 372):

> God loves from Whole to Parts; but human soul
> Must rise from Individual to the Whole:
> Self-love but serves the virtuous mind to wake,
> As the small pebble stirs the peaceful lake;
> The centre mov'd, a circle strait succeeds,
> Another still, and still another spreads,
> Friend, parent, neighbour, first it will embrace,
> His country next, and next all human race,
> Wide and more wide, th' o'erflowings of the mind
> Take ev'ry creature in, of ev'ry kind;
> Earth smiles around, with boundless bounty blest,
> And heav'n beholds its image in his breast.

This *is* a sublime passage, with its fusion of the double motion of human love outwards and upwards and of divine love downwards and inwards, till the image of Heaven is reflected in the human breast. One equates the human breast with the lake, described earlier in the passage, into which the small pebble of self-love is dropped to ripple out into ever-widening circles of social love, and which can be thought of as reflecting not only 'Heav'n', the sky above, but 'Earth' that smiles around. Love of God is also love of the world He has created. This *is* mystical, though Pope's cosmos – unlike Wittgenstein's value-free 'everything that is the case' – embodies the values of benevolent and inclusive all-pervading order and organisation. Pope feels that one can speak clearly enough of this sense of the mystical (no doubt it is not the deepest sense), at least for poetic purposes; he has no feeling that one should be silent about it. If the greatest modern poetry is based on a 'rage for order' in chaotic times, modern poets ought to find this unfashionable, didactic *Essay on Man* very congenial reading.

Yet I am left reflecting that, however splendid his cosmic panorama, however beguiling his vision of ultimate harmony, Pope lacks the muscle of a really strong thinker. I am moved by *An Essay on Man* as a vision of a harmony that may be, that might be; he is not strong enough to win me over to a vision of a harmony that is. If he was not a great thinker, he was a man of feeling, a true poet of friendship, and if one can excuse a warmth that verges almost on idolatry (and forget all one knows about the posed theatricality of Bolingbroke's actual character), one will prefer the tribute to Bolingbroke which succeeds the passage Mack so much admires. (It is to be found in Epistle IV, lines 373 to 390). This passage does not aim at the 'sublime', unless there is a sublime of courtesy. It expresses, however, that mixture of unfeigned awe and warm friendship which, in Pope's poetry as a whole, is the deepest and truest emotion:

> Come then, my Friend, my Genius, come along,
> Oh master of the poet, and the song!
> And while the Muse now stoops, or now ascends,
> To Man's low passions, or their glorious ends,
> Teach me, like thee, in various nature wise,
> To fall with dignity, with temper rise;
> Form'd by thy converse, happily to steer
> From grave to gay, from lively to severe;
> Correct with spirit, eloquent with ease,
> Intent to reason, or polite to please.
> Oh! while along the stream of Time thy name
> Expanded flies, and gathers all its fame,

Say, shall my little bark attendant sail,
Pursue the triumph, and partake the gale?
When statesmen, heroes, kings, in dust repose,
Whose sons shall blush their fathers were thy foes,
Shall then this verse to future age pretend
Thou wert my guide, philosopher, and friend?

6

Moral Essays: Pope as a Moral Philosopher

Pope conceived *An Essay on Man* as part of a much longer philosophical poem which would be called *Ethic Epistles*. (Pope's original title, kept by Mr F. W. Bateson in the Twickenham edition is *Epistles to Several Persons*, though on his death-bed he agreed with Warburton, to whom he left the task of preparing a complete posthumous edition, that the poems should be called *Moral Essays*.) If *An Essay on Man* seems to a modern reader superficial in its reasoning, the ethic epistles are, from the view of modern moral philosophy, even more disappointing. Modern philosophical essays bristle with interesting questions. It seems generally agreed, for instance, that if some state of being or kind of experience is good or desirable, that fact in itself does not impose any duty on anybody to pursue it; it is nobody's duty, for instance, to read Shakespeare's sonnets or see Giorgione's 'La Tempesta', in the Accademia in Venice. It is everybody's duty to pay for his ticket on the bus, to keep promises, to tell the truth, though the result of not paying one's bus ticket is trivial (one can rely on other people paying for theirs) and the result of keeping a promise (to buy a bottle of whisky for an alcoholic) or telling the truth (admitting to one's wife that one has long ceased to love her) may increase the sum of un-happiness in the world. There is also the interesting point that some-thing may be one's duty if it is an act logically but not psychologically possible to do (it is logically possible for a full-blooded and susceptible man to resist the advances of a woman whom he finds very attractive and who flings herself into his arms in conditions of complete con-venience and privacy).

Ethics in Pope's time was anything but the intellectually amusing study it has become now, and the interest of the ethic epistles lies almost solely in Pope's examples of the various types of conduct that spring from various types of psychological bias, or 'ruling passion', not to more than the slightest degree in his thoughts. There are some abstract points, however, that are interesting as being typical of Pope's age. Virtue and benevolence to him deserve praise, and are therefore beyond what we call doing one's duty (we do not praise a man for paying his debts, though we blame him if he fails to do so). Happiness, for Pope, in its highest sense, is something well beyond comfort and contentment and certainly beyond calm sensual satisfaction; it is a kind of exaltation of the soul that accompanies the habitual practice of virtue. Good sense, wit, judgment, are more closely connected with virtue for Pope than they are with modern moral philosophers, and folly is more closely connected with vice. Finally, Pope is on the verge of being a determinist: he feels that our conduct is determined by our characters (for which, at their roots, we are not of course responsible), but this determinism does not prevent him from praising wise and virtuous conduct and condemning foolish and vicious conduct in a very whole-hearted way.

Warburton, perhaps, had this excuse for choosing the title *Moral Essays* instead of *Epistles to Several Persons*. His title suggests a direct connection, which exists, with *An Essay on Man*, a connection quite lacking for instance in one of Pope's greatest poems, later than the *Moral Essays*, the *Epistle to Dr Arbuthnot*: this is a poem not on an abstract topic but rather a sort of condensed autobiography on the whole course and pattern of Pope's life, and on his motives and excuses for being a poet – an *apologia pro vita sua*. The four ethic epistles, on the other hand, are abstract: one on the characters of men, another on the characters of women, one on the use of riches (with reference to parsimony, greed, prodigality, and character) and the fourth also on the use of riches, but with reference especially to the errors of taste prevalent in building great houses and designing gardens. This last, the earliest published, is addressed to Pope's friend Burlington, the introducer of the Palladian style and, with Kent's new intimate style in landscape-gardening in mind, attacks the old type of symmetrical garden. Though it will be dealt with later in more detail, for its satirical power, it is worth mentioning here as a revelation of Pope's own taste which reflects itself as much in his poems as in the kind of buildings and gardens he preferred.

Lord Burlington was not himself a great architect and his little Roman villa at Chiswick is a pleasant toy. Pope was not fair to the burly and manly English baroque style of Wren, Hawksmoor, and Vanbrugh. The romantic gardens at Stourhead are the loveliest in

England, but the elegant and slightly mechanical symmetries of the house do not impress themselves on the memory. Almost all readers of today, however, will agree with Pope in preferring the artificial wildness of Kent, who, working on a comparatively small scale, is more intimate than 'Capability' Brown, to the symmetrical garden, with its mirror-image balancings (ironically, so like the balancings of some of Pope's own couplets) of Versailles or Hampton Court. Pope's prose is sometimes, though rarely, more memorable than his verse and in the *Epistle to Burlington* he has two striking separate notes on a single couplet:

> One boundless Green, or flourish'd Carpet views,
> With all the mournful family of Yews . . .

These are lines 95 and 96 of the poem. Pope's notes are:

95. The two extremes in parterres, which are equally faulty; a *boundless Green*, large and naked as a field, or a *flourished Carpet*, where the greatness and nobleness of the piece is lessened by being divided into too many parts, with scrolled works and beds, of which the examples are frequent.

The second note is:

96. Touches upon the ill taste of those who are so fond of Evergreens (particularly Yews, which are the most Tonsile) as to destroy the nobler Forest-trees, to make way for such little ornaments as Pyramids of dark-green, continually repeated, not unlike a Funeral procession.

'Tonsile' means easily clipped or shorn. Yews lend themselves easily to topiary work and Pope would not have approved of the taste of a friend of mine who has turned one of his yews into a baby elephant and the other into a knight on horseback. (In a smaller garden, however, than Pope was envisaging, such tricks can be amusing.) What is interesting, however, is that in this first-published *Moral Essay* (to accept for the moment Warburton's term) the interest seems more in aesthetics than in ethics. Timon's villa, indeed the main target of the satirical part of the poem, is attacked for its ostentatious display of wealth as well as for its bad taste; but presumably the display would have been just as selfish had Timon's taste, by Pope's standards, been perfect.

In the two general essays, on the characters of men and women,

Pope was dealing with subjects perhaps lending themselves less to poetic fantastication and charm than the subject of taste in the *Epistle to Burlington*, but of more widely human interest: the mysterious springs of human motivation and the hidden consistencies that give pattern to an otherwise inexplicable life. Each man is driven by a 'ruling passion' which he is often unaware of possessing; but this shows itself in the 'strongest' actions of his life and often nakedly on his death-bed.

The essay on 'The Knowledge and Characters of Men' is addressed to Richard Temple, Viscount Cobham, and illustrated by brilliant character sketches. Pope appeals to Cobham as a man who knows the world and knows that men cannot be judged by books, by moral theorising, alone. Pope's reply to this attack on the mere theorist is that we cannot judge men merely by our own observations, which may have an unconscious bias, and that we need some general framework of ideas to guide us. But our task remains difficult:

> And yet the fate of all extremes is such,
> Men may be read, as well as Books too much.
> To Observations which ourselves we make,
> We grow more partial for th' observer's sake;
> To written Wisdom, as another's, less:
> Maxims are drawn from Notions, these from Guess.
>   There's some Peculiar in each leaf and grain,
> Some unmark'd fibre, or some varying vein:
> Shall only Man be taken in the gross?
> Grant but as many sorts of Mind as Moss.

Pope judges the difficulty of observing others exactly by the great difficulty of knowing and making a fair estimate of our own motives:

> Oft in the Passions' wild rotations tost,
> Our spring of action to ourselves is lost:
> Tir'd, not determin'd, to the last we yield,
> And what comes then is master of the field.
> As the last image of that troubled heap,
> When Sense subsides, and Fancy sports in sleep,
> (Tho' past the recollection of the thought)
> Becomes the stuff of which our dream is wrought:
> Something as dim to our internal view
> Is thus, perhaps, the cause of most we do.

Pope seems almost to anticipate Freud here. Having thus stated so beautifully the complexity and perhaps the impossibility of either self-knowledge or knowledge of others, Pope nevertheless discovers his over-simple, but satisfying – poetically satisfying – solution to it, the theory of the 'ruling passion'. He illustrates this by a real dazzling young man, who seemed all contradictions, Philip Duke of Wharton:

> Wharton, the scorn and wonder of our days,
> Whose ruling Passion was the List of Praise;
> Born with whate'er could win it from the Wise,
> Women and Fools must like him or he dies;
> Tho' wond'ring Senates hung on all he spoke,
> The Club must hail him master of the joke,
> Shall parts so various aim at nothing new?
> He'll shine a Tully and a Wilmot too.

(Marcus Tullius Cicero, the eloquent, unfortunate Roman statesman, and John Wilmot, Earl of Rochester, rake, wit, drunkard, and occasionally superlative lyric or satirical poet.)

> Then turns repentant, and his God adores
> With the same spirit that he drinks and whores;
> Enough if all around him but admire,
> And now the Punk applaud, and now the Fryer.
> Thus with each gift of nature and of art,
> And wanting nothing but an honest heart;
> Grown all to all, from no one vice exempt,
> And most contemptible, to shun contempt;
> His Passion still, to covet gen'ral praise,
> His Life, to forfeit it a thousand ways;
> A constant Bounty which no friend has made;
> An angel Tongue, which no man can persuade;
> A Fool, with more of Wit than half mankind,
> Too quick for Thought, for Action too refin'd;
> A Tyrant to the wife his heart approves;
> A Rebel to the very king he loves;
> He dies, and out-cast of each church and state,
> And (harder still) flagitious, yet not great!
> Ask you why Wharton broke thro' ev'ry rule?
> 'Twas all for fear the Knaves should call him Fool.

This fine passage shows us what Aristotle meant by poetry being truer than history; it is not even in key facts the real Wharton. It is doubtful, for instance, whether anybody but his old, ugly mistresses ever 'loved' George I. But the portrait has a consistency and a dramatic impact lacking in the real Wharton; it reminds us of a kind of politician recurrent in history, made for success and courting disaster, Lord Randolph Churchill, Sheridan, Charles James Fox, Pope's own beloved Bolingbroke. Cobham, a good-natured man of easy morals but a passionate patriot, is similarly made a recurrent type in the last four lines, in one of those sincere and spontaneous compliments in which (as Hazlitt recalls Lamb remarking) Pope excelled:

> And you! brave COBHAM, to the latest breath
> Shall feel your ruling passion strong in death:
> Such in those moments as in all the past,
> 'Oh, save my Country, Heav'n!' shall be your last.

The epistle to Cobham, as befits its subject and the man it was addressed to, has more solidity but less charm and variety than 'Of the Characters of Women' directed (though not, out of propriety, naming her) to Pope's dearest woman friend and possibly mistress, Martha Blount. It has the airiness and gaiety that attracted Pope in the world of women; in spite of his passionate admirations for his men friends, he was most at ease perhaps as a woman's man. But women, if as open as men to his compliments, were no more free of his sting. Yet he never tired of their indefinable volatility:

> Come then, the colours and the ground prepare!
> Dip in the Rainbow, trick her off in Air,
> Chuse a firm Cloud, before it fall, and in it
> Catch, ere she change, the Cynthia of this minute . . .

> Strange graces still, and stranger flights she had,
> Was just not ugly, and was just not mad;
> Yet ne'er so sure our passion to create,
> As when she touch'd the brink of all we hate . . .

> If QUEENSBERRY to strip there's no compelling,
> 'Tis from a Handmaid we must take a Helen . . .

That graceful impudence takes us back almost to the world of *The Rape of the Lock.*

Pope first of all quotes and accepts a saying once let drop by Martha, 'Most women have no characters at all.' They are so soft and

changeable that there is no defining them, there is no single aim they
seem to pursue. He changes his mind. All women have in fact two
passions: for love, in the plainest physical sense; and for what ruling
Chaucer's Wife of Bath called 'the maistrye' – for mastery or dominion
over their men-folk. Yet he turns this accusation into a kind of
compliment. To call a woman a rake, a term confined usually in
Pope's time to the successful, attractive and daring male libertine,
gives women something of a masculine dash and swagger. Prudish
moralising seems as much out of place in one case as in the other. To
say that every woman would be a Queen seems to impute to her a
very high and glittering ambition. Finally to say that men's ruling
passions sometimes let them off the hook, but women's never, seems
to attribute to women a single-minded drive that men might envy:

> Men, some to Bus'ness, some to Pleasure take;
> But ev'ry Woman is at heart a Rake:
> Men, some to Quiet, some to public Strife;
> But ev'ry lady would be Queen for life.

One wishes that was all there was to say. But there was something
womanish in Pope himself and women should beware women. The
following lines, the most brilliant in the poem, are also the most
chilling and terrifying:

> Pleasures the sex, as children Birds, pursue,
> Still out of reach, yet never out of view,
> Sure, if they catch, to spoil the Toy at most,
> To covet flying, and regret when lost:
> At last, to follies Youth could scarce defend,
> 'Tis half their Age's prudence to pretend;
> Asham'd to own they gave delight before,
> Reduc'd to feign it, when they give no more:
> As Hags hold Sabbaths, less for joy than spight,
> So these their merry, miserable Night;
> Still round and round the Ghosts of Beauty glide,
> And haunt the places where their Honour dy'd.
>   See how the World its Veterans rewards!
> A youth of frolicks, an old Age of Cards,
> Fair to no purpose, artful to no end,
> Young without Lovers, old without a Friend,
> A Fop their Passion, but their Prize a Sot,
> Alive, ridiculous, and dead, forgot!

Each line, almost each half-line, is a slap in the face.
But these are imaginary beings and Pope's spite could, alas, be
more personal and more unjust. Mrs Howard, Countess of Suffolk,
had been a good friend to Pope and remained a very loving friend to
Martha Blount, even after this poem was published. With many
things to make her miserable, she was one of the most charming and
obliging women in England. She was a little deaf. The husband from
whom she was separated was a brute. George II, whose mistress she
was, was a boor and hardly pretended to care for her. Queen Caroline,
to whom she was Maid of Honour, delighted in forcing her to
perform humiliating services. Nevertheless, the better side of Pope
spoke justly of her in a short poem written well before the epistle:

I know a thing that's most uncommon;
    (Envy be silent and attend!)
I know a Reasonable Woman,
    Handsome and witty, yet a Friend.

Not warp'd by Passion, aw'd by Rumour,
    Nor grave thro' Pride, or gay thro' Folly,
An equal Mixture of good Humour,
    And sensible soft Melancholy.

'Has she no Faults then (Envy says) Sir?'
    Yes, she has one, I must aver:
When all the World conspires to praise her,
    The Woman's deaf, and does not hear.

What can have changed Pope's tone? Lady Suffolk was very
absent-minded and Pope had been at a dinner party when he heard
her ask her footman to remind her to send a message to ask after the
health of Martha Blount, perhaps her dearest friend, who was ill.
People attempting to excuse Pope at the time of publication said that
he took some but not of course all of the characteristics of Henrietta
Hobart (so Mrs Howard had been born). But one doubts this. The
woman in 'Of the Characters of Women' uncannily resembles the
poised and good-natured woman of the short complimentary poem,
the poise and good-nature now seen as springing from a fundamental
heartlessness:

'Yet Chloe sure was formed without a spot –'
Nature in her then err'd not, but forgot.
'With every pleasing, ev'ry prudent part,

Say, what can Chloe want?', – she wants a Heart.
She speaks, behaves, and acts just as she ought;
But never, never, reach'd one gen'rous Thought.
Virtue she finds too painful an endeavour,
Content to dwell in Decencies for ever.
So very reasonable, so unmov'd,
As never yet to love, or to be lov'd.
She, while her Lover pants upon her breast,
Can mark the figures on an Indian chest;
And when she sees her friend in deep despair
Observes how much a Chintz exceeds Mohair.
Forbid it Heav'n, a Favour or a Debt
She e'er should cancel – but she may forget.
Safe is your Secret still in Chloe's ear;
But none of Chloe's shall you ever hear.
Of all her Dears she never slander'd one,
But cares not if a thousand are undone.
Would Chloe know if you're alive or dead?
She bids her Footman put it in her head.
Chloe is prudent – would you too be wise?
Then never break your heart when Chloe dies.

The last line for me has rather a horrible effect; as if strong and light
hands that had been playfully but with growing speed and malice
stroking a green twig should suddenly snap it in half.

Two other portraits, added by Pope in 1744 though written long
before, distress by their cruelty. Philomedé is a brutal picture of a
drunken nymphomaniac of high rank with intellectual pretensions.
Many critics have thought her modelled on Henrietta Churchill, the
eldest daughter of the great Duke of Marlborough, Countess Godol-
phin, later Duchess of Marlborough in her own right, the great friend
and reputedly the lover of Congreve. It is doubtful whether the
creator of Millamant could have loved such a woman as Pope describes,
and F. W. Bateson in the Twickenham Edition finds other reasons
for finding the case against Henrietta Churchill 'not proven'. Atossa
is a picture of a great lady driven almost mad by her own temper; she
was once thought to be Sarah, Duchess of Marlborough, but Bateson
gives convincing reasons for identifying her with the Duchess of
Buckinghamshire, who had quarrelled with Pope and made it up but
who infuriated him by leaving in 1743 her letters, including some of

Pope's, to Pope's enemy Lord Hervey. Madness should not be mocked:

No Thought advances, but her Eddy Brain
Whisks it about, and down it goes again,

And if Philomedé *was* Henrietta, the coarse obviousness of

What then? Let Blood and Body bear the fault,
Her Head's untouch'd, that noble Seat of Thought,
Such this day's doctrine – in another fit
She sins with Poets thro' pure Love of Wit,

belies the woman who could charm the great Congreve in his last years and who deserved more courtesy. Yet in spite of these passages we must agree with Warburton 'that there is nothing in Mr Pope's works more highly finished than this epistle'.

There are these sour tastes. But the moral feeling is redeemed by the tender concluding address to Martha Blount. Even Warburton, who hated Martha (she inherited money and property from Pope that he would have liked himself), feels bound to admit that on Pope's death-bed 'it was very observable . . . that Mrs Blount's coming in gave a new turn of spirits or a temporary strength to him'. Whether Martha was ever Pope's mistress, in the physical sense, hardly seems to matter. Vivacious and kind, though never strikingly intelligent, she was in a more important way the wife in everything but name of an invalid of genius. He could not have done without her presence in his later years, on his visits to great houses, as companion and nurse. He left her £1,000 (a much grander sum than it is today), his goods and chattels, and a life-interest in his estate, which she enjoyed till her death in 1763. She never married.

Here are the lines to Martha:

And yet, believe me, good as well as ill,
Woman's at best a contradiction still.
Heav'n, when it strives to polish all it can
Its last best work, but forms a softer Man:
Picks from each sex, to make its Fav'rite blest,
Your love of Pleasure, our desire of Rest,
Blends, in exception to all gen'ral rules,
Your Taste of Follies, with our Scorn of Fools,
Reserve with Frankness, Art with Truth ally'd,
Courage with Softness, Modesty with Pride,

Fix'd Principles, with Fancy ever new;
Shakes all together, and produces – You.
  Be this a Woman's Fame; with this unblest,
Toasts live a scorn, and Queens may die a jest.
This Phoebus promis'd (I forget the year)
When those blue eyes first open'd on the sphere;
Ascendant Phoebus watch'd that hour with care,
Averted half your Parents simple Pray'r,
And gave you Beauty, but deny'd the Pelf,
Which buys your sex a Tyrant o'er itself.
That gen'rous God, who Wit and Gold refines,
And ripens Spirits, as he ripens Wines,
Kept Dross for Duchesses, the world shall know it,
To you gave Sense, Good Humour, and a Poet.

The ordinary reader need not perhaps bother himself with the complicated details about the alteration to the text of the four *Moral Essays* in the 1744 edition of Pope's works, worked on before his death with Warburton, and approved by Pope before his death, but perhaps approved very much under Warburton's pressure. The best account of the whole matter is F. W. Bateson's preface to the Twickenham edition of *Epistles to Several Persons*. Though the Chloe passage – Pope oddly spelt the name Cloe – was a last-minute addition, it came out in Pope's own edition of his *Works* (vol. II, part II) dated 1738, but not on sale till 1739. Bateson takes the fact that Pope and Mrs Howard were still alive as evidence that the character can be only partly based on Mrs Howard, but I am not convinced; when we recognise part of a literary character as modelled on reality there is no clear line we can draw between fact and fiction. Henrietta, though she remained as loyal a friend to Martha as ever, must have been profoundly hurt. Like the passage on Henrietta, 'The Epistle to Burlington', the earliest written, was polished up a great deal in Pope's lifetime. Pope agreed to add the Atossa and Philomedé passages on his death bed and also agreed to re-arrange the blocks of verse in the Bathurst and Cobham epistles and alter them to dialogue (Cobham complained that he had not been given any good lines). Warburton was no doubt exerting undue pressure on the dying Pope but in any case the Bathurst and Cobham poems are on the dullish side, and do not compare with the two masterpieces, the epistles to Burlington and Martha Blount. Bateson, in a word, rather exaggerates the importance and disastrousness of Warburton's interference.

The epistle to Bathurst, on the use of riches, is, as I say, rather dull. Few of us are tempted to practise miserliness, a neurotic condition rather than a vice, and therefore not a proper object of satire: fewer of us still have the opportunity to practise prodigality. Yet the passage on the results of this vice, the account of the death of the second Duke of Buckingham of the Villiers line – the author of *The Rehearsal* and Dryden's Zimri in *Absalom and Achitophel* – still has something of the vivid and concrete sense of the sordid which Pope's last great successor, George Crabbe, was at the end of the eighteenth and the beginning of nineteenth century to bring to the heroic couplet:

> In the worst inn's worst room, with mat half-hung,
> The floors of plaister, and the walls of dung,
> On once a flock-bed, but repair'd with straw,
> With tape-ty'd curtains, never meant to draw,
> The George and Garter dangling from that bed
> Where tawdry yellow strove with dirty red,
> Great Villers lies – alas! how chang'd from him,
> That life of pleasure, and that soul of whim!
> Gallant and gay, in Cliveden's proud alcove,
> The bow'r of wanton Shrewsbury and love;
> Or just as gay, at Council, in a ring
> Of mimick'd Statesmen, and their merry King,
> No Wit to flatter, left of all his store!
> No Fool to laugh at, which he valu'd more.
> There, Victor of his health, of fortune, friends,
> And fame; this lord of useless thousands ends.

I have corrected, though using Mr Bateson's edition as my main source here, his interesting miscopying 'type-ty'd', which might have come into his head or his secretary's from the laboriousness of copying verse on the typewriter. 'Villers' for 'Villiers', on the other hand, is correct phonetically and is still how this distinguished family pronounces its surname. The rest is wearisome. A criminal like Colonel Francis Chartres is a villain of too deep a dye to be the object of satire. And Pope's example of a virtuous use of wealth, John Kyrle of Ross-on-Wye in Herefordshire, somehow lacks colour. Out of an income of £500 a year Kyrle provided his neighbours with drinking fountains, wayside seats, almshouses, roadside trees, and regular distributions,

G

which he handed out personally, of bread to the poor. Public benefactors rarely make a strong personal impression and though he lived
to be ninety, dying in 1724, Kyrle was when Pope died remembered
only as the Man of Ross.

The epistle to Burlington, of which a sketch has been already given,
is on the other hand Pope at his most glitteringly brilliant. It is about
the misuse of riches in gratifying false taste. The grand central set
piece is the description of Timon's villa – Pope is thinking of Timon
in his days of luxury and lavishness, not in his time of disillusioned and
misanthropic poverty. This piece caused a scandal, for it was very
widely taken as typical of Pope's ingratitude. The Duke of Chandos
had built a great house called Cannons, surrounding it with old-
fashioned formal gardens, near Edgware. Chandos had been kind and
hospitable to Pope at Cannons, and he wrote to Pope that he took no
offence and did not see any attack on himself in the passage: though
at the same time he wrote to his friend Anthony Hammond (he
differed from Pope's Timon in at least being aware that taste in
building was not his great strength): 'I am not so ignorant of my own
weakness, so as not to be sensible of its Justice in some particulars.'
It was not, however, quite a matter of a straight attack as in the
distressing passage in the Martha Blount epistle on Mrs Howard.
Pope's Timon was a generalised and imaginary character, typical of
the ostentation of any vain and rich man. Cannons may have contributed some characteristics to Timon's villa but so might many
great houses in the English baroque style of building and with the
balanced formal gardens,

> Another age shall see the golden Ear
> Imbrown the Slope, and nod on the Parterre,
> Deep Harvests bury all his pride has plann'd,
> And laughing Ceres re-assume the land.

The parterre is the level grassy space in a garden which today we call
the lawn. It was ornamented with flower-beds, and Pope disliked these
when they were too regularly distributed, but at the same time an open
clipped parterre, with no flower-beds, seemed to him too much like a
shaven meadow. The slope for him was not a natural slope but an
artificial construction, like military earthworks banked round fortifi-
cations. Both 'golden' and the verb 'imbrown' suggest the colours of a
painting by Claude rather than those of nature. Laughing Ceres, in
reassuming the land, resumes, as goddess of fertility, her former

sovereignity, and the personified deep harvests, purposefully burying all that Timon's pride has planned, seem like her attendant labourers. Even such a clear and forceful passage as this in Pope demands, for its full appreciation, awareness of such niceties.

Chandos died in 1744, Cannons was sold in 1747, pulled down, and Warburton, still annotating a new edition, exults that Pope's prophecy has come true; though Pope almost in a flurry had earlier denied any intention of giving offence, and Chandos, wryly admitting to a friend that some strokes might be just, had blandly denied to Pope taking offence. About the Augustan age, with its boasts of candour, there was sometimes something very devious.

7
Pope as a Satirist

Of all the genres that make up the Western literary tradition, satire is the only form invented by the Romans rather than the Greeks. (In the Middle Ages, it might be claimed that the sustained allegory, like Dante's *Divine Comedy*, the romance in verse or prose, the lyric idealisation of romantic love even its hopelessness and agony, and the miracle and morality play are all new inventions, but something like parallels to all of them can be found in the classical world; even the most centrally important of literary forms since the mid-eighteenth century, the realistic novel, has a somewhat scabrous ancestor in Petronius's *Satyricon*.)

Though this mistake was often made by seventeenth century critics, our word 'satire' has nothing to do with Greek satyrs or the satyr plays, short farces which were often put on for light relief after the performance of a Greek tragedy. The 'old comedy' of Aristophanes, with its frank ridicule of actual living persons like Socrates and its relevance to current political and social situations, was what we would call satirical, but the Greeks did not.

The Latin noun from which our word derives is *satura*, a medley, often used of *satura Lanx*, a dish containing a variety of cooked meats and vegetables, a sort of *olla podrida*, and *satura* is related to *satur*, full, *satis*, enough, and *saturare*, to fill to the brim or saturate. In Horace's satires and epistles, the idea of a medley, of *sermo* or chat, a ranging conversation on a variety of topics, is just as important as satire in the stricter sense (later to be developed from 'comical' satire in Horace to 'tragical' satire in Juvenal) whose main aim is to castigate, and thus correct, the prevailing follies and vices of the age, In his direct *Imitation of Horace* and in poems in the Horatian manner like one of Pope's great poems, the *Epistle to Dr Arbuthnot*, the idea of a range of light, varied, interesting and informal conversation is just as important to Pope as strictly satirical denunciation or mockery. Some of the best passages in Pope's Horatian satires (*The Dunciad*, comic, powerful, and nasty, and sometimes beautiful and sublime, is quite another matter) are paradoxically hardly satirical in the narrower sense at all. Pope's purpose in the Horatian satires seems often, though not always, less the correction of the age than the dazzling display of his own various wit and the sympathetic revelation of his temperament. Unlike *The Dunciad*, the Horatian satires are on the whole the poems of a man who desires to be liked, who has explanations for his occasional ebullitions of spleen, who sees, amiably, the ridiculous side in himself and his friends as well as his enemies, than the poems of a man who desires above all to hurt and to be feared.

The great natural satirist of the age was not Pope but his friend Swift. Swift was a more disappointed man than Pope, and tougher in his personal rancours, but, against the grain of his own temperament, he lashes the vice and not the man. In *Gulliver's Travels*, for instance, there are some personal allusions in Lilliput, but we can enjoy the satire on the pettiness of political intrigue and ambition without tracing these. Swift had three main objects of attack: the growing taste for useless luxury for the few rather than for decent plenty for the many (Pope, as Timon's Villa shows, could satirise luxury but as *The Rape of the Lock* shows he had a sneaking liking for it, too); the pursuit of pedantic and useless knowledge in the arts and sciences (one of Pope's topics in *The Dunciad*, but Pope would have hesitated to attack the Royal Society as a body, and was always ready to praise Newton, whose discoveries lacked the direct human usefulness – making two leaves of grass grow where one grew before – which was all that Swift demanded of science); and the folly of human pride in reason. Man for Swift is an animal *capax rationis* rather than *rationale*, though when, like the Yahoos, he gives up every effort to control his passions and appetites rationally he declines into something lower than the beasts (the Yahoos are degenerate, not primitive, human beings). The reasoning horses have no passions to control and are therefore, unlike the benevolent Portuguese sea-captain who befriends Gulliver, not fit models for man. And Gulliver in the end is the most absurd creature in the book, his pride totally misplaced, as he prances and whinnies like a horse and thinks therefore that he is a wholly rational creature. Pope makes conventional attacks on pride but has a dangerous kind of pride himself:

Yes, I am proud; – I must be proud to see
Men not afraid of God, afraid of me . . .

The two great men and great friends were, though they did not realise it, temperamentally opposite. Temperamentally respectful to great lords, powerful statesmen, learned lawyers, courtly manners, Pope could never have said like Swift that he hated all trades and professions but loved his neighbour. Swift hated show and glory; Pope liked it to be known that he had numbered Oxford and still numbered Bolingbroke or Peterborough among his great friends, that he had friends like Mrs Howard at George II's court, had dined with Sir Robert Walpole however much he deplored his policies, moved in the best circles. Swift, during the short period when he had written pamphlets for the Tories, had been interested in the real sources of power not its outward elegances. The wretched poverty of Ireland was enough to destroy any desire for luxury. The growth of wealth and luxury through the expansion of trade, which Pope had celebrated in *Windsor Forest*, was one of the things which the essentially anti-Augustan Swift hated. His ideal was simplicity, stoic virtue, the older Roman republic; Cincinnatus called from his plough to be dictator, Scipio roasting turnips at his Sabine farm, the rustic, plain honesty of a time well before Augustus.

Pope, on the other hand, was a petted invalid, depending very much on expensive small sensualities: lampreys cooked in a silver pot, the aroma of strong coffee to clear his wits, or a dram of spirits (which he would call for even at dinner with his grand friends) to disperse his headaches. Pope's five acres of rented ground at Twickenham, joined under the road by a grotto glittering with mineral spars, were not really a Republican farm, nor were the broccoli, chickens (bred by himself) and the fine-flavoured roast mutton from Banstead downs on which he 'piddled round the year' – pecked at, with a tiny appetite – really a poor man's dinner. Swift cared for none of these things, rationing himself to a pint of cheap wine a day, and serving decent but very plain dinners at his Deanery. Among his Ireland of rustic squires and country clergymen, Swift might find more plentiful eating and particularly drinking, but there was nothing of the 'great world' he had had his brief taste of in London. The disease which he suffered from, Ménière's syndrome, bringing on deafness, giddiness, and fits of nausea, did not attract him more strongly to the world. Pope, on the other hand, even when he was very ill, loved not only the glitter and the gold but the gauze and the tinsel. Only the mutual recognition of genius could draw together such mighty opposites.

A great satirist should also, like Swift or like Dr Johnson in *London* and *The Vanity of Human Wishes*, take a rather grim and limited view of the possibilities of happiness in this life. In *An Essay on Man* and the *Moral Essays* Pope had taken a very sanguine and cheerful view of the power of reason to regulate passion and the tendency, implanted by God Himself, of our natural self-love, the spring of all our energies, to grow into social love. He did not, as the greatest satirists tend to, see his age even at its best as a period of mixed blessings. He loved London as the great centre of all the pleasures and amenities of life. His moral excuse for the savageries of *The Dunciad* was that he was defending a high civilisation against forces of stupidity and corruption that were threatening to destroy it. By contrast, Swift, living in Dublin, with wretched poverty, injustice, bigotry, fanaticism, brutish cruelty all around him, did not feel that he was existing at the centre of a high civilization, and looked on the social world and on the roots and fruits of human action with a much harsher eye.

Pope therefore lacked both Swift's scepticism about the values of the world at its most polished and Swift's sense as a Christian clergyman that he had a duty to love his neighbour, however boring and common-place, as himself. Pope, indeed, reserved a considerable portion of his income for charity; but it was charity of an impersonal sort. Pope had been admired since his teens but Swift had, till his thirties, faced the prospect that he might die either as the secretary of a grandee of polished minor talent, Sir William Temple, or a curate in a remote Irish parish. But Swift's early poverty and dependence, like Johnson's, had given both a respect for the common drab fate of man, which was outside Pope's range. Swift had in the end been offered a consolation prize, the Deanery of St Patrick's (since Queen Anne would not give the author of *A Tale of a Tub*, that effective but irreverently farcical defence of the Anglican establishment against the creeds of Geneva and Rome, an English or even an Irish bishopric), a consolation prize which exiled Swift from all his dearest friends.

Yet Swift had a far more bitter mind than Pope's but also a far more just one. Some of Pope's best writing in his satires is invective against his enemies or compliments to his friends, poetry that has all the eloquence of true feeling but little of the balance of just thought. Other pieces of excellent writing in Pope's satires, but in their kind outside the bounds of satire proper, are in the nature of an emotional auto-biography; a kind of apology, as in the Arbuthnot poem, for a life shut up in literature because it could have no other outlet, an apology that veers effectively between the gaily self-mocking, the proud, and the sad.

The Horatian poems are also lightened by passages of sheer skittish gaiety, as when the heavy-footed would-be epic poet, Sir Richard Blackmore, is mentioned:

> What? Like Sir *Richard*, rumbling, rough, and fierce,
> With ARMS, and GEORGE, and BRUNSWICK crowd the Verse?
> Rend with tremendous Sound your ears asunder,
> With Gun, Drum, Trumpet, Blunderbuss & Thunder?
> Or nobly wild, with *Budgell*'s Fire and Force,
> Paint Angels trembling round his *falling Horse*?

There are no trembling angels in Budgell's flattering and absurd address to George II in 1728: but Pope is quite justified (as, according to Voltaire, men would be if there were no God) in inventing them. Spleen can be dispersed by hearty laughter.

Pope was perhaps not the ideal imitator of Horace. The mark of Horace's satires and epistles, Sir Herbert Grierson once suggested, is a quiet amenity; the mark of Pope's imitations is rather a restless brilliance, and Cowper in his conversational poems is perhaps more genuinely Horatian in tone. Horace felt genuine admiration for the court of Augustus and for Augustus's advisers like Maecenas. Pope felt hatred and contempt for the stupid boorishness of George II; almost or actual physical loathing for Lord Hervey, the go-between between Sir Robert Walpole (whom George II hated), Queen Caroline (who could persuade her husband to adopt Walpole's sensible policies), and the King; and a mixed feeling of admiration and disgust for Sir Robert himself, the coarse, capable spreader of corruption. Pope's abstract political principles were not very coherent. *Windsor Forest* reflects his admiration for the peace policy of the Tories, Bolingbroke and Harley; in the hands of a Whig like Walpole, however much prosperity he brings to the country, a peace policy becomes another sign of timidity, sloth, old England's decay. Here and there, as in this instance, the tone of the satires seems to reflect a desperate sadness – something personal to Pope, and not really rising from what he is writing about – which has little to do with the manner of Horace or the state of England. These are only pretexts.

There is another way in which Pope profoundly differs from Horace. It shows itself chiefly in *The Dunciad*, which does not of course claim to be a Horatian poem. *The Dunciad* is a mock-epic strangely touching the grandeur of a real epic: a terrible celebration of the power of chaos. But there are touches of the mood I mean even in the Horatian poems. I would describe it as a latent fear of madness. If Pope had not been able to project his almost overwhelming disgust with the conditions of his own physical existence, its squalor and pain, into the final revised *Dunciad* in Four Books he might have gone mad. The complete *Dunciad*, a sublime, terrible, truncated poem, all the machinery of a real epic and none of the action – for it is the business of the Goddess of Dulness to impede action, not further it – is a myth into which Pope projects and gives form to the darkness and chaos of his deepest inner self.

But there are hints of an uneasy awareness of an uncomfortably close connection between poetry and madness in even the most various and lively of the purely Horatian poems, an *Epistle to Dr Arbuthnot*:

> Shut, shut the door, good *John*! fatigu'd I said,
> Tye up the knocker, say I'm sick, I'm dead,
> The Dog-Star rages! Nay, 'tis past a doubt,
> All *Bedlam*, or *Parnassus*, is let out . . .

Sirius, the dog-star, appears in late summer: it is dangerous, in the ascendant, to sanity (one thinks both of mad dogs and madmen). But it was in the late summer, under Sirius, that the Romans held their public recitals of poetry. The *Epistle to Dr Arbuthnot* is an apologia for Pope's career as a poet. Poetry in his own case at least is a sane diversion not a mad obsession. It springs from what was early recognised by the best judges of the young poet's time as a true gift, not from an illusion:

> Why did I write? what sin to me unknown
> Dipt me in ink, my Parents' or my own?
> As yet a Child, nor yet a Fool to Fame,
> I lisp'd in Numbers, for the Numbers came.
> I left no Calling for this idle trade,
> No Duty broke, no Father dis-obey'd.
> The Muse but serv'd to ease some Friend, not Wife,
> To help me thro' this long Disease, my Life,
> To second ARBUTHNOT! thy Art and Care,
> And teach, the Being you preserv'd, to bear.

(Arbuthnot, remembered for his prose political satire, *John Bull*, was also a very distinguished doctor of medicine and Pope's personal

physician as well as close friend.) Pope then enumerates his early
encouragers:

> But why then publish? *Granville* the polite,
> And knowing *Walsh*, would tell me I could write . . .

'Polite' in the eighteenth century was an adjective not confined to social
agreeableness but included a mastery of the arts and the more pleasing
parts of literature (mere dry scholarship, like Bentley's greatness in
classical textual criticism or Theobald's reading in minor Elizabethan
and Jacobean drama was not 'polite learning').

Pope goes on to enumerate some more distinguished (and in fact
slightly later) admirers, St John, the great Congreve, Swift. He is
making a good case that he is walking not in Bedlam but on Parnassus,
the mountain of the Muses – 'tis a pleasing air', said John Locke, the
most prosaic of English philosophers, whose flat common sense
dominated English thought in Pope's age, 'but a barren soil'. Pope
pleads the excuses, for being a poet, of early talent, lack of other duties,
a harmless diversion in a life of pain, putting his work into print only
by the advice or with the approval of the best judges. Yet eloquent and
justly famous as these words addressed to Arbuthnot are, no sensitive
reader can miss an inner uneasiness: *qui s'excuse, s'accuse.*

However one reads these lines they are very unlike satire in the
narrower and more usual sense. The same could be said of these quietly
moving lines from Pope's imitation of the first poem in Horace's first
book of epistles: a poem addressed, like *An Essay on Man* to Bolingbroke. It begins with a passage of mildly sad reproach. Like all of us,
Pope has 'done those things he ought not to have done, and left undone
those things that he ought to have done':

> Long, as to him who works for debt, the Day;
> Long as the Night to her whose love's away;
> Long as the Year's dull circle seems to run,
> When the brisk Minor pants for twenty-one;
> So slow th'unprofitable Moments roll,
> That lock up all the Functions of my soul;
> That keep me from Myself; and still delay
> Life's instant business to a future day:
> That task, which as we follow, or despise,
> The eldest is a fool, the youngest wise;
> Which done, the poorest can no wants endure,
> And which not done, the richest must be poor,

If one finds satire there it is merely that daily gentle self-reproach that is such a pervading element in the mind of a mature and sane man that he hardly notices its presence.

Yet there is satire in the conventional sense in Pope's brisk acknowledgment that wisdom like that is hardly wisdom for the world:

> 'Tis the first Virtue, Vices to abhor;
> And the first Wisdom, to be Fool no more.
> But to the world, no bugbear is so great,
> As want of figure, and a small estate.

I am not sure, however, whether one should call the end of this epistle to Bolingbroke satire or not. It echoes the end of *An Essay on Man*, repeating even the great phrase about Bolingbroke as Pope's 'guide, philosopher and friend'. But the tone is no longer one of idolatrous awe but one of affectionate but sometimes slightly tart raillery.

Bolingbroke was one of those figures in English politics, like Lord Randolph Churchill, Rosebery, or Curzon, in whose histories a short flash of glory or disaster is followed by a short or long period of decline (or in Curzon's more bitter case under Lloyd George by an apparent re-elevation to great office with a deprivation of real power). There are various possible attitudes, of varying dignity, towards this predicament and Bolingbroke and Rosebery were probably the wisest of this group in affecting to be absorbed in literary pursuits (for which both had a real talent) and to disdain the power they had let slip and could not hope to grasp again. But Bolingbroke has less dignity than Rosebery in that he still wished to meddle in the game and still longed for a prize beyond his reach. Pope's Horatian epistle addressed to him was written in 1737. Bolingbroke had really permanently ruined his political prospects by fleeing in an unnecessary panic to France in 1715 to the court of the Old Pretender. He left the Pretender's court after the failure of the 1715 rising (he was never a man to attach himself to a broken cause) and was allowed, by the reversal in 1725 of a Bill of Attainder against him, to return to England and inherit property. His political rights were not restored and he was at first cold-shouldered both by the Tory Jacobites, who felt he had betrayed their cause, and the Tory Hanoverians, loyal to the memory of his rival, Oxford.

But these old feuds were becoming out of date and Bolingbroke attached himself to the clever group of young politicians, Chesterfield, Pulteney, and others, who hung round the Prince of Wales's court and were united mainly by hopes of office when the prince succeeded, and by hatred of Walpole. As a writer in *The Craftsman*, Bolingbroke was a polished and effective critic of Walpole. But Walpole had spotted that his showy, though shadowy, rival lacked political courage. He threatened impeachment and Bolingbroke fled again to France, once again panicking in a crisis. His political prospects were ruined. Even our memory of their friendship is spoiled by his attack on Pope in 1749 for an earlier clandestine printing of Bolingbroke's *The Patriot King*, of more copies than Bolingbroke had authorised him to print, with alterations in the text not authorised at all. Bolingbroke has been much blamed for this attack by those who have not read it. Pope, even if his ultimate intentions were good, was a devious little man. Bolingbroke's attack, considering all the circumstances and the fiery temper of a sick and embittered old man, was restrained: there was no justifying Pope, who had broken his word and altered another man's manuscript; the best that Warburton can do is to attribute to Pope generous motives based on the feeling that Bolingbroke had both undervalued and failed to give the final polish to a masterpiece. One dwells on all this because Bolingbroke was the one great romantic friendship of Pope's life. His greatest admirer among the younger politicians, Chesterfield, wrote sadly:

> He has been a most mortifying instance of the violence of human passions, and of the weakness of the most improved and exalted human reason. His virtues and his vices, his reason and his passions, did not blend themselves by a gradation of tints but formed a sudden and shining contrast. Here the darkest, there the most splendid colours; and both rendered more striking from their proximity.

Bolingbroke died in his early seventies, isolated and in pain, in 1751. It is a little consoling, when one thinks how much he meant to Pope, that his attack of 1749 was reasonably moderate in tone and that some memories of friendship and admiration lingered.

Pope, since *An Essay on Man*, had perhaps learned by 1737 to love his great friend this side of idolatry. What he most reproaches Bolingbroke with is a lack of sympathy in some deep emotional or mental trouble of Pope's. Pope, in 1733, had boasted of not being able to be pinned down, not being a partisan. The passage comes in the

Epistle to Fortescue, an imitation of the first satire in Horace's second book:

My Head and Heart thus flowing thro' my Quill,
Verse-man or Prose-man, term me which you will,
Papist or Protestant, or both between,
Like good *Erasmus* in an honest Mean,
In Moderation placing all my Glory,
While Tories called me Whig, and Whigs a Tory.

By 1737 he is beginning to wonder whether this 'incoherence', this inability to take a simple and straightforward stand about anything is not perhaps a sign of madness, the madness that threatens all poets. Bolingbroke is reproached because, fussing over a friend's clothes, he does not see into a friend's heart:

You laugh, half Beau half Sloven if I stand,
My Wig all powder, and all snuff my Band;
You laugh, if Coat and Breeches strangely vary,
White Gloves, and Linnen worthy Lady Mary!
But when no Prelate's Lawn with hair-shirt lined,
Is half so incoherent as my mind,
When (each Opinion with the next at strife,
One ebb and flow of follies all my Life)
I plant, root up, I build, and then confound,
Turn round to square, and square again to round;
You never change one muscle of your face,
You think this Madness but a common case,
Nor once to Chanc'ry, nor to Hales apply;
Yet hand your lip, to see a Seam awry!
Careless how ill I with myself agree;
Kind to my dress, my figure, not to Me.

Hales was the Doctor of Bedlam, though he had died nine years before in 1728 (Pope, as often, may have been tessellating old pieces of writing, making fragments of different periods into a new whole); Pope would have had to be made a Ward in Chancery, if he were sent to Bedlam. Certainly, he did not want to be sent to Bedlam; the reproach is a tender one, but it does hint at an obtuseness in Bolingbroke, the splendid egoist, to a friend's most agonising inner troubles.

Pope continues, and perhaps Bolingbroke, as he read on, felt growingly uncomfortable. In the tone of polite raillery he must have noted

that some of the raillery was all too apt, some of the politeness undeserved. Yet he was as friendly as ever when he saw Pope on a hurried
visit to England in 1738. He wept at Pope's death-bed in 1744 (Walpole
had fallen from power in 1742, and it was safe for Bolingbroke to
resettle at home). Yet this whole passage subtly deflates the godlike
image of Bolingbroke that concludes *An Essay on Man*. Good-natured
banter is of course a proper Horatian tone; but just how good-natured
is Pope really being here?

> Is this my Guide, Philosopher, and Friend?
> This, He who loves me and who ought to mend?
> Who ought to make me (what he can, or none,)
> The Man divine whom Wisdom calls her own,
> Great without Title, without Fortune bless'd,
> Rich ev'n when plunder'd, honour'd while oppress'd,
> Lov'd without youth, and follow'd without power,
> At home, tho' exil'd, free, tho' in the Tower,
> In short, that reas'ning, high, immortal Thing,
> Just less than Jove, and much above a King,
> Nay half in Heav'n – except (what might seem odd)
> A fit of Vapours clouds this demi-God.

One finds in these lines, in which affection struggles with bitterness, a perception of a certain hollowness with a lingering wish to
adore, the coincidence of 'Vapour' and 'Vapours', of that 'reas'ning.
. . . Thing' and 'the Reas'ning *Engine*' of the most powerful lines of
Lord Rochester's *Satyr against Mankind*, one of the few great poems of
the Restoration other than those of Milton and Dryden:

> Reason, an *Ignis fatuus*, in the Mind,
> Which leaving light of Nature, sense behind;
> Pathless and dang'rous wand'ring ways it takes
> Through errors Fenny-*Boggs*, and Thorny *Brakes*;
> Whilst the misguided follower, climbs with pain,
> *Mountains* of Whimseys, heaped in his own *Brain*:
> Stumbling from thought to thought, falls head-long down,
> Into doubts boundless Sea, where like to drown,
> Books bear him up awhile, and makes him try,
> To swim with Bladders of *Philosophy*;
> In hopes still t'oretake th' escaping light,
> The *Vapour* dances in his dazled sight,

Till spent it leaves him to eternal Night,
Then Old Age, and experience, hand in hand,
Lead him to death, and make him understand,
After a search so painful and so long,
That all his Life he has been in the wrong;
Hudled in dirt, the reas'ning *Engine* lyes,
That was so proud, so witty, and so wise.

The first half of Rochester's eloquent passage recalls Pope's sense, in the first half of his own moving address to Bolingbroke, that nothing

Is half so incoherent as my Mind,
When (each opinion with the next at strife,
One ebb and flow of follies all my Life)
I plant, root up, I build and then confound,
Turn round to square, and square again to round . . .

In the second half of both passages, Pope's

In short, that reas'ning, high, immortal Thing,

seems to express with less direct force and scorn, but with more lingering sadness, what cuts killingly home in Rochester's terrific line:

Hudled in dirt, the reas'ning *Engine* lyes . . .

Rochester expresses that Hobbesian pessimism and atheism which Pope had rejected in *An Essay on Man* in favour of the great chain of being, the doctrine of plenitude, cosmic optimism, the ultimate identity of self-love, social-love, and obedient adoration of God. Perhaps, Pope did not at all times quite convince himself and had, like his own Atossa, an 'Eddy Mind'. (I leave it to the philosophical historians to say whether or not the way Charles II's courtiers, and even some of his more cynical divines, like Marvell's enemy Archdeacon Parker, took Hobbes or aspects of him was or was not a misinterpretation of the 'good old man', whom, as Aubrey tells us, the Bishops wanted to burn.)

Pope's streaks of sadness may have been due to another view of man's place in the chain of being, again strongly expressed by Rochester: are we so much morally superior to the animals and do they exist merely for our use? Is our lot happier than theirs?

For Hunger, or for Love, they fight, or tear,
Whilst wretched *Man* is still in Arms for fear;

For fear he armes, and is of Armes afraid,
By fear to fear, successively betrayed,
Base fear, the source whence his best passions came,
His boasted Honor, and his dear bought Fame . . .

This, I think, was never Pope's philosophy but it expressed a constant danger in the background: something into which he feared that the great Augustan civilisation, which he associated particularly with the short period of Harley's and Bolingbroke's Tory government at the end of Queen Anne's reign, might degenerate, through corruption, into the chaos and night that is depicted in *The Dunciad*. Sometimes he seems to feel a ferocity and despair almost like Rochester's, but he expresses it more cautiously. He clears himself, in the first dialogue of his two-part *Epilogue to the Satires*, of any suspicion of personal rancour against Sir Robert Walpole:

Friend: . . . And where's the Glory? 'twill be only thought
The Great man never offer'd you a Groat.
Go see Sir ROBERT –
  Pope: See Sir ROBERT! – hum –
And never laugh – for all my life to come?
Seen him I have, but in his happier hour
Of Social Pleasure, ill-exchan'd for Pow'r;
Seen him, uncumber'd with the Venal tribe,
Smile without Art, and win without a Bribe.
Would he oblige me? Let me only find,
He does not think me what he thinks mankind.
Come, come, at all I laugh He laughs, no doubt,
The only diff'rence is, I dare laugh out.

Pope could, thus, be courteous enough to Walpole as a person in whom no doubt he recognised a coarse but warm good nature (Walpole used to sit at his dinner-table, over the port when the ladies had gone, talking bawdy, as the only subject at which all men feel themselves on a level) and an easy, almost lazily dominating power of mind. Perhaps Walpole suffered in the eyes of Pope, Swift, and all the surviving wits of Harley's and Bolingbroke's short heyday for not taking much pleasure in reading or in the company of men of letters and instead devoting his wealth and his very considerable knowledge and taste to collecting pictures for his great house at Houghton.

Pope, nevertheless, treats Walpole personally with good nature, politeness, appreciation of his real personal attractiveness. But the passage is followed immediately by one of Pope's most direct attacks, on the corrupt policies of the Prime Minister. His sword is now drawn and he stabs without chivalry. Corruption the Whore is an obvious portrait of Walpole's mistress (whom he married, when set free by his wife's death), Molly Skerrett:

Lo! at the Wheels of her Triumphal Car,
Old *England*'s Genius, rough with many a Scar,
Dragg'd in the Dust! his Arms hang idly round,
His Flag inverted trails along the ground!
Our Youth, all liv'ry'd o'er with foreign Gold,
Before her Dance; behind her crawl the Old!
See thronging Millions to the Pagod run,
And offer Country, Parent, Wife, or Son!
Hear her black Trumpet thro' the land proclaim
That 'Not to be corrupted is the Shame.'
In Soldier, Churchman, Patriot, Man in Pow'r,
'Tis Avarice all, Ambition is no more!
See, all our Nobles begging to be Slaves!
See, all our Fools aspiring to be Knaves!
The Wit of Cheats, the Courage of a Whore,
Are what ten thousand envy and adore.
All, all look up, with reverential awe,
On Crime, that scape, or triumph o'er the Law:
While Truth, Worth, Wisdom, daily they decry –
'Nothing is Sacred now but Villany.'

Yet may this Verse (if such a Verse remain)
Show there was one who heard it in disdain.

This, surely, is the sublime of satire, grand in style and noble in political courage. Contrast poor Bolingbroke, fleeing to France in fear of impeachment for his much milder attacks in *The Craftsman*, revisiting England furtively and briefly in 1738, planning to settle at home only in 1742, when Walpole had fallen and Bolingbroke had at last inherited the property of his long-lived father. A far better judge of men than the great political rhetorician, Pope, no doubt estimated correctly – as in 1735 Bolingbroke had failed to – that he had nothing to fear from Walpole.

But courage is only one quality of these Horatian poems. No group gives us more glimpses of the troubled inner man or displays more variously the range of tone 'from grave to gay, from lively to severe'. The unifying quality is Pope's exultant sense of his own poetic power. The conclusion of his marvellously funny epistle to Augustus (George II is praised with the utmost decorum for his lack of every kingly quality) reveals both his contempt for George, who will not have enough penetration to see that he is being ridiculed, and his amused delight in the buzzing swarm of Grub Street flatterers who spatter George II with Birthday Odes:

> Besides, a fate attends on all I write,
> That when I aim at praise, they say I bite.
> A vile Encomium doubly ridicules;
> There's nothing blackens like the ink of fools;
> If true, a woful likeness, and if lyes,
> 'Praise undeserved is scandal in disguise':
> Well may he blush, who gives it, or receives;
> And when I flatter, let my dirty leaves
> (Like Journals, Odes, and such forgotten things
> As Eusden, Philips, Settle, writ of Kings)
> Cloath spice, line trunks, or flutt'ring in a row,
> Befringe the rails of Bedlam and Sohoe.

Praise undeserved *is* scandal in disguise and George II must be more of a fool than Pope thinks to mistake such blatant irony as this:

> Oh! could I mount on the Maeonian wing,
> Your arms, your Actions, your Repose to sing!
> What seas you travers'd! and what fields you fought!
> Your Country's Peace, how oft, how dearly bought!

The mock praise of the King puts George himself into the court of the goddess Dulness and looks forward to Pope's final revision of *The Dunciad*, his last great achievement. The King, like the goddess, brings a stupefying sleep to everything and everybody within the range of his influence. The policy of peace which Pope made so much of in *Windsor Forest* was now become the policy of expensive inaction and sloth:

> How barb'rous rage subsided at your word,
> And Nations wonder'd while they dropp'd the sword!

How, when you nodded, o'er the land and deep,
Peace stole her wing, and wrapt the world in sleep . . .

Physical courage (with, perhaps, his tetchy devotion to his shrewd wife
Caroline on whom he depended for guidance, and for physical love,
and whom he perpetually bullied and nagged) was perhaps George II's
only virtue. He showed his mettle at Oudenarde and later, at Dettingen,
was the last English King to risk his life in battle. The policy of peace,
in which he was guided by his wife and Walpole, built up England's
strength and prosperity. But we do not look in satire for the balance
of a scholarly historian like J. H. Plumb; and in literature the laughers
have the last word.

Pope himself thought of *The Dunciad* as a similarly gay poem. The
satire, he said, was not made for the sake of the authors castigated in
it; the authors were made for the sake of the satire. The Twickenham
editor, Professor James Sutherland, seems to accept this view, though
he emphasises the obscurity and heaviness of what was to become
Book Four, *The New Dunciad* of 1742. Behind the cloudiness, he sees
the growing influence of the pedantic Warburton, in some ways the
evil genius of Pope's last years, who combined an inept aspiration towards philosophical profundity with a muddled over-ingenuity, most
strikingly displayed in the notes, in his ambitious edition of Shakespeare, which Dr Johnson tore to pieces. Certainly, many of Warburton's footnotes cast darkness rather than light on the text and
Thomas Gray, the most learned poet of his age, confessed he found
much of Book Four impenetrable.

Yet Book Four cannot be dismissed. If it contains the most obscure,
it also contains the most sublime passages of *The Dunciad*. The sublime
is often obscure, and a poem which celebrates the coming triumph of
Dulness, the coming reign of Chaos and Old Night, which ends with
the line

And Universal Darkness buries all.

cannot have the light, quick modulation of tone that makes the
Horatian poems perpetually amusing, however much bitterness they
conceal. For me, Book Four, however dark it is in some places, raises
The Dunciad as a whole (the final version of October 1743, with Cibber
substituted for Theobald as the hero) to a new level. It ceases to be a
mock-epic, or even an anti-epic. In its own strange way it becomes, in
its most weighty and yet soaring passages, as grand as Milton.

I have described the origins of *The Dunciad* and the circumstances of Pope's revisions and additions. I seek here, by selected quotations and comments, to illustrate its poetic quality. We shall have then done with Pope's work in verse (his prose, in passing, has had all the attention which in a brief study like this it deserves). A final short chapter will deal, in a fairly summary way, with the ups and downs of Pope's posthumous reputation.

The Dunciad, if one contrasts it with the swift and delicate miniature action of Pope's other mock-epic *The Rape of the Lock*, might remind us more (in mood also, perhaps) of Samuel Beckett's *Waiting for Godot* where 'nothing happens, twice'. It has all the heavier paraphernalia of the epic poem, the invocation to the Muse, the introduction of the hero, the descriptive list of subsidiary heroes, the competitive games which are at once an imitation of serious action and a relaxation from it (though, with its totally supine Theobald-Cibber hero, *The Dunciad* has no serious action to be relaxed from), the recapitulation of past events that led to the present situation (the need for the dull poets of the past to have a successor worthy of Dulness's divine approbation), and the final triumph of the goddess.

Yet, in spite of my allusion to *Waiting for Godot*, one cannot describe *The Dunciad* as an epic of non-action. In a parody of the style of the great Dr Bentley, in his notes on Greek and Latin poems and in his wild transformation of *Paradise Lost*. Pope writes:

> . . . Dulness here is not to be taken contractedly for mere
> Stupidity, but in the enlarged sense of the word, for all Slowness
> of Apprehension, Shortness of Sight, or imperfect Sense of things.
> It includes . . . Labour, Industry, and some degree of Activity and
> Boldness: a ruling principle not inert, but turning topsy-turvy the
> Understanding, and inducing an Anarchy or confused State of
> Mind. This remark ought to be carried along with the reader
> throughout the work . . .

The design of the poet, to illustrate the power of Dulness, is therefore, according to the feigned Bentley, a grand and sublime one: if the characters are mean, Pope is not primarily concerned with 'killing flies' but

> sports with a nobler quarry, and embraces a larger compass; or
> (as one saith, on a like occasion)
> *Will see his Work, like Jacob's ladder, rise,*
> *Its foot in dirt, its head amid the skies.*

Though the notes attributed to the feigned Bentley are intended to make fun of him (and though Pope makes very good fun of him, in verse, in Book Four) one feels also that he has a reluctant respect for Bentley. 'It is a pretty poem, Mr Pope, but you must not call it *Homer'* is the sort of remark that one finds it hard to forgive but hard, also, to treat with mere contempt. It would be typical of Pope's devious way of doing things ('by indirections find directions out') to mock Bentley and yet let Bentley give the main clue to what *The Dunciad* is aiming at.

Yet it remains true that not quite nothing but almost nothing in the sense of real epic, or mock-epic, action is presented. In the First Book, in the final 1743 version, Dulness is invoked, her academy and special seminar cell for poets near Bedlam described, 'The Cave of Poverty and Poetry' and we are told about the four Cardinal Virtues she instils in her votaries: Fortitude, or indifference to just criticism: Temperance, or willingness to starve if one may continue to scribble: Prudence, or keeping a weather eye open for the libel laws: and, in lines too good to summarise,

Poetic Justice, with her lifted scale,
Where, in nice balance, truth with gold she weighs,
And solid pudding against empty praise.

The hero, Cibber, or rather a queer miscellaneous character who is mostly Cibber but also the remains of Theobald, is then introduced. Pope retains the library of Theobald, the pedantic scholar, though Cibber rarely opened a book except to crib a plot from Molière. His *The Non-Jurer* is a crude adaptation to English circumstances of *Tartuffe*. Desperate about how to earn a living (though, from his early days as an actor and hack-playwright Cibber was comfortably off), Cibber is now raising an altar, and setting fire to a propitiatory offering of his own worst plays and miscellaneous writings.

Dulness douses the fire, initiates Cibber into her secrets, and carries him to court to be announced successor of the dead poet laureate Eusden. He is proclaimed King of the Dunces and in Book Two his accession to the throne is celebrated by epic games. There is a race to catch a phantom poet who disappears on being caught; celebrations of tickling or flattering, vociferating or writing polemically on any side for money; and a diving competition into the filth of the Thames, illustrating both the grovelling nature of the Grub Street poet and the art of sinking in poetry. It was the scatological nature of this passage, and of similar passages in the Fourth Book of *Gulliver's Travels*, that particularly disgusted Dr Johnson. It must be said on Swift's and Pope's behalf (though I share Johnson's feelings) that such imagery is very effective for expressing contempt: one is likely to hear the exclamation 'Shit!' these days from the lips of the best-bred young woman. There was a long tradition of scatological humour in literature and Pope and Swift may have been using the tradition, not writing out of a Freudian anal erotism, a surviving infantile obsession with their own excrement. Book Two ends with a competition to stay awake while prose by 'Orator' Henley and verse by Sir Richard Blackmore is read aloud: nobody wins, all the Dunces fall asleep, and stagger off to their sordid rest.

In Book Three, Dulness conveys Cibber to her Temple and, as he lies with his head on her lap, gives him a vision of the past Empire of Dulness and its future prospects. Like Gibbon dealing with the Goths, the Huns, and later the rise of Islam and of the Mongol Hordes, Pope, as if weary of the cult of reason and civilisation, lights up his evocation of barbarism with a strange, pure poetry: Dulness is speaking:

'How little, mark! that portion of the ball,
Where, faint at best, the beams of Science fall.
Soon as they dawn, from Hyperborean skies
Embody'd dark, what clouds of Vandals rise!
Lo! where Maeotis sleeps, and hardly flows
The freezing Tanais thro' a waste of snows,
The North by myriads pours her mighty sons,
Great nurse of Goths, of Alans, and of Huns!
See Alaric's stern port! the martial frame
Of Genseric! and Attila's dread name!
See the bold Ostrogoths on Latium fall;
See the fierce Visigoths on Spain and Gaul!
See, where the morning gilds the palmy store
(The soil that arts and infant letters bore)
His conqu'ring tribes th'Arabian prophet draws,
And saving Ignorance enthrones by Laws.
See Christians, Jews, one heavy sabbath keep,
And all the western world believe and sleep. . . .'

This strange passage has few of the effects we habitually associate with satire. The hordes from what Wordsworth later called 'the frozen loins of the North' have the proper port of heroes: Pope thought the couplet

> Lo! where Maeotis sleeps, and hardly flows
> The freezing Tanais thro' a waste of snows,

the most musical he ever wrote. The music, which we can hear (though Dr Johnson could not), comes from a skilful use of hiatus, 'Mae-o-tis', 'Tan-a-is', 'thro' a'; from echoing long vowels, 'sleeps', 'freezing'; perhaps from the contrast of the shortish vowel of 'hardly' in '*hardly* flows' with the long vowel of 'waste', further lengthened by two final consonants, in a 'wa*st*e of snows'. (The initial semi-vowel 'w' also helps: a 'haste of snows' or a 'taste of snows', supposing that either were possible for sense, would ruin the sound.)

Pope, in fact, when he reaches Book Three, and the vision that is presented to Cibber, is often indulging himself less in satire proper than in a pleasant kind of musical delirium:

> But in her Temple's last recess inclos'd,
> On Dulness' lap th'Anointed head repos'd.
> Him close she curtains round with Vapours blue,
> And soft besprinkles with Cimmerian dew.
> Then raptures high the seat of Sense o'erflow,
> Which only heads refin'd from Reason know.
> Hence, from the straw where Bedlam's Prophet nods,
> He hears loud Oracles, and talks with Gods:
> Hence the Fool's Paradise, the Stateman's Scheme,
> The air-built Castle and the golden Dream,
> The Maid's romantic wish, the Chemist's flame,
> And Poet's vision of eternal Fame.

This is a madman's vision, yet it has an odd kind of crazy prettiness.

Let us consider that perverse attractiveness. 'Cimmerian dew' (besides the implied pun on Cibber) reminds us of Ovid's Cave of Sleep. The 'Vapours blue' have a prettiness in their colour; in the catalogue of follies none of us is utterly hostile to the air-built Castle of the Maid's romantic wish or to the Golden Dream (if we make this wider than the alchemist's quest for gold, and the quite separate mention of the chemist's flame suggests we might). Pope himself was not indifferent to the vision of eternal Fame. We wonder how far the line

> Which only heads refin'd from Reason know

is pure sneer, how far unconscious wistfulness: an obscure sense in Pope of one path in life and poetry he has never explored. Such uncertainties give *The Dunciad* as a whole a power alien to that which we usually associate with satire.

In the Fourth and final Book (originally published separately as *The New Dunciad*) there is again no epic action. Simply, the Goddess Dulness, by the mere force of her inertia, triumphs over all intelligent, concerted human effort. The universities cease to study things or ideas, become busy simply with words (a little like the structuralist linguisticians, critics, and philosophers of today). Young noblemen on the Grand Tour learn only the luxuries of vice and find 'All Classic learning lost on Classic ground'. If they find indolence irksome they will be encouraged to become virtuosos, studying butterflies, shells, birds' nests, moss, so long as their learning leads them to no wide and general views on Nature or Nature's God. Or they will be lured into collecting useless, and perhaps forged, antiquities; again without enlarging their minds. Those who have graduated in this course of folly are given degrees and partake of a sacramental cup administered by the Goddess's Magus. A long speech by the Goddess ends in a supernatural yawn which gradually spreads universal slumber. All sense of order, hierarchy, and mutual obligation is lost. Chaos and Old Night inherit the earth, as before God imposed the Cosmic Order. Universal darkness buries all.

The tone is sombre: but at its most sombre, as in the conclusion, sublime. There is elsewhere something more attractive than sublimity, there is beauty, as in these lines that might remind one of those already quoted from Book Three and Tanais and Maeotis:

Before her, *Fancy*'s gilded clouds decay,
And all its varying Rain-bows die away,
Wit shoots in vain its momentary fires,
The meteor drops, and in a flash expires.
As one by one, at dread Medea's strain,
The sick'ning stars fade off th' ethereal plain;
As Argus' eyes by Hermes' wand opprest,
Clos'd one by one to everlasting rest;
Thus at her felt approach, and secret might,
Art after *Art* goes out, and all is Night.

The whole ten lines are memorable and delightful. But the couplets about Medea and Argus are something more, they have a thrilling beauty, a strange fusion of lamentation and triumph, that might remind one of Keats's *Ode to Melancholy*. There is a similar Keatsian colouring in the passage on the Grand Tour though with, at the beginning and end, a very unKeatsian satiric bite:

> To happy Convents, bosom'd deep in vines,
> Where slumber Abbots, purple as their wines;
> To Isles of fragrance, lily-silver'd vales,
> Diffusing languour in the panting gales:
> To lands of singing, or of dancing slaves,
> Love-whisp'ring woods, and lute-resounding waves.
> But chief her shrine where naked Venus keeps,
> And Cupids ride the Lyon on the Deeps;
> Where, eased of Fleets, the Adriatic main
> Wafts the smooth Eunuch and enamour'd swain.

The reference of course is to the Venetian Republic in the century of her elegant decay, and remaining rococo creativeness, the century of Tiepolo, Guardi, Canaletto, masked balls and formal gallantries, the Venice of Byron's *Beppo* and Browning's 'A Toccata of Galuppi's'. Pope could say like Browning's speaker, 'I was never out of England . . .', but like him Pope has caught the place. When we read such a passage, we are not to approve or even to tolerate; but Pope feels, as we feel, the dangerous, decadent charm.

I shall not quote the grand concluding lines of the poem, Miltonic in their grandeur. They are too familiar for comment, though their force and eloquence can never weary. My final suggestion to the reader is that *The Dunciad* is something much more than the description given it by a fine young critic, Mark Jacobs, a poem that holds one's attention by being at once broadly comic and strikingly nasty. I do find much that is boring and disgusting in the First and Second Books. In the Third and Fourth Books, Pope raised satirical poetry to a grandeur, and found place in it for a sensuous richness, that had never marked the form before and was never to mark it again. *The Dunciad* is hard to criticise because there is no other work sufficiently similar to compare it with profitably. It is probably the most powerful and original of all Pope's poems, but also the least charming; where elsewhere he always seems to write with ease, here one is conscious of recurrent triumph but also of continual effort. Certainly, it is not my own, or probably anybody's, favourite poem of Pope's; unlike the Horatian Imitations and the *Moral Essays* it is not companionable. But its final form is both a dying man's victory over distress, humiliation, and weakness and the most unequivocal piece of evidence, among all Pope's writings, of his ability to display in a long poem steady, sustained, and sometimes majestic power.

8
Pope and the Critics

Pope begins his epistle to Bathurst with the teasing question:

> Who shall decide, when Doctors disagree,
> And soundest Casuists doubt, like you and me?

Pope's reputation rests even today in that undecided state: a state in which according to the Jesuits (readers of Pascal will remember) if, of two contrary opinions held by learned Doctors, a man follows the one that suits his taste and temperament, he is safe. But let us fine down the nature of the disagreement. No competent critic has ever denied that Pope is among our great writers, if not our great poets, and only Blake has denied that he is a master of versification. In our own time, however, F. W. Bateson, a notable Blake scholar, insists that far from being a perfect poet within strict limits, Pope is a brilliant but singularly uneven writer. He aimed, on Walsh's advice, at 'correctness'; but even a cursory reader will notice that he has the technical fault of repeating the same rhymes at too short intervals. But many great poets have technical weaknesses: the still unsettled question about Pope is whether his undeniable greatness is properly that of a poet.

In 1756, only twelve years after Pope's death, this question was first raised by Joseph Warton, in the first of two volumes on Pope, the second and less daring and interesting of which appeared in 1782. Like many writers who are the first to raise a question, and who have not the stimulus of contrary argument to force them to refine on it, Warton puts the case more bluntly and concisely than it has been put since. Here is the core of his question:

> We do not, it should seem, sufficiently attend to the difference there
> is betwixt a man of wit, a man of sense, and a true poet . . . For one
> person who can adequately relish and enjoy a work of imagination,

113

twenty are found who can taste and judge of observations on familiar life and the manners of the age . . . The sublime and pathetic are the two chief nerves of all genuine poesy. What is there transcendently sublime or pathetic in Pope?

Warton's point about 'observations on familiar life and manners' was first properly taken up in an edition of Pope of 1806 by the Reverend William Lisle Bowles, whose early sonnets had delighted Coleridge. Bowles's argument is in line with some points made by Wordsworth in the preface to *Lyrical Ballads*. In 1819, Bowles finds himself still having to defend his preface; Byron, one of the nineteenth century's two great admirers of Pope (the other was Ruskin) had attacked Bowles with contempt and insolence. Bowles, keeping his temper, writes in 1819:

> The plain course of my argument [of 1806] was simply this:
> First, *Works of nature*, speaking of those *more* beautiful and sublime, are *more* sublime and beautiful than works of art, therefore more poetical. Second. The passions of the human heart, which are the same in all ages, and which are the causes of the sublime and pathetic in sentiment, are more *poetical* than *artificial manners*.

In the high Victorian age, Matthew Arnold, himself always a touching and pleasing and sometimes a great poet, and certainly a great critic, saw that these worn old counters of the sublime, the pathetic, the beautiful, the natural, the artificial, were no longer current coin. 'High seriousness' is a more cloudy but also a more comprehensive term than 'the sublime'. The idea of poetry as a 'criticism of life' allows for an element of strenuous thought in great poetry. It also allows for poetry to probe questioningly into the limited and thwarting conditions of our existence (like Arnold himself in 'Dover Beach'), in a way that concepts like 'natural' and the 'artificial' – a poem would not be a poem unless it were an artifice, and 'nature' in an unhelpfully broad range of senses has to be its content or subject-matter – or talk about 'the passions of the human heart which are the same in all ages' do not. With an infinitely subtler mind, Arnold nevertheless instinctively shared Bowles's dislike of Pope.

Arnold therefore takes Pope when he is being light, chatty, and trivial (it would have been much fairer, since he was looking for poetic 'touchstones', to take the last couplet of *The Dunciad*):

They hand, great Anarch! lets the curtain fall;

And Universal Darkness buries All.

and sets against Pope in a chatty vein three lines from Shakespeare, Milton, and Chaucer chosen for their concentrated weight and echoing depth of feeling. It is like proving that the Betjeman of 'Miss Joan Hunter Dunn' is not in the same league as the Eliot of 'Marina' or the Yeats of 'In Memory of Eva Gore-Booth and Con Markiewicz'. Betjeman might justly reply that this was not intended to be that sort of poem, nor was it the only sort of poem he could write.

Here is Arnold on Pope:

Do you ask me whether Pope's verse, take it almost where you will, is not good?

To Hounslow Heath I point, and Banstead Down;
Thence comes your mutton, and these chicks my own.

I answer: Admirable for the purposes of the high priest of an age of prose and reason. But do you ask me whether such verse proceeds from men with an adequate poetic criticism of life, from men whose criticism of life has a high seriousness, or even, without that high seriousness, has a poetic largeness, freedom, insight, benignity? Do you ask me whether the application of ideas to life in the verse of these men, often a powerful application, no doubt, is a powerful *poetic* application? Do you ask me whether the poetry of these men has either the matter or the inseparable manner of such an adequate poetic criticism; whether it is the accent of

Absent thee from felicity awhile . . .

or of

And what is else not to be overcome . . .

or of

O martyr sounded in virginitee!

I answer: it has not and cannot have them; it is the poetry of the builders of an age of prose and reason. Though they may write in verse, though they may in a certain sense be masters of the art of versification, Dryden and Pope are not classics of our poetry, they are classics of our prose.

Arnold is talking throughout of 'these men' because he is equating Dryden, the very different poet of a very different age, with Pope. His example from Dryden is the opening of *The Hind and the Panther*:

A milk-white hind, immortal and unchanged,
Fed on the lawns and in the forest ranged.

How with any honesty he could describe this hauntingly beautiful couplet as typical of the founder of an age of prose and reason I cannot see. My criticism is almost the opposite. When we realise that the milk-white hind is an allegorical representation of the Roman Catholic Church the couplet for me loses a little – but only a little – of its magic. In any case, the allegorical form looks backward to Spenser and the Middle Ages, not forward to Pope. If the choice from Dryden is obtuse, the Pope choice seems to me (I hope not deliberately) blatantly unfair. The proper criticism of the couplet about the mutton and the chicks is that its tone is, even for that conversational verse in a light tone which has flourished since Horace and flowers independently in Chaucer, a little on the trivial and self-indulgent side. It should not be presented as Pope at his best *even in that particular manner.* Yet Arnold had perhaps the most persuasive *voice* of all our critics; and I have been appalled by the number of sensitive, charming, and well-read people who still take his judgment on Pope for gospel.

Arnold deals with Pope in his famous lectures *On Translating Homer,* where he is both fairer and – probably for that very reason – more genuinely formidable. He pointed out that the English heroic couplet, whether Pope or anybody else had been using it, tended of its nature to pair and separate off things that are not paired or separated off in Homer. But he allows Pope something of Homer's swiftness and praises Pope's gift for dealing with elevated passages, like the Sarpedon passage on the preferability of noble death in action to slow natural decay, which Pope first attempted as a boy. He feels, nevertheless, that Pope, because of his obsession with style, cannot render plain narrative:

Homer invariably composes 'with his eye on the object', whether the object be a moral or a material one: Pope composes with his eye on the style, into which he translates his object, whatever it is.

All this was discussed here in the chapter on Pope and Homer. The conclusion was that though Pope does not render the 'material object' very palpably, his style has more 'flexibility' than Arnold allows, can handle straight narrative (a good example, though there was no space to cite it, might have been the touch of comedy in the *Iliad* of the first confrontation of Paris by Menelaus) and does have his eye on the 'moral object'. That is to say: Pope reflects by subtle adjustments of style Homer's changing moods as a poet, and the changing emotions of his character. Gerard Manley Hopkins, a much greater poet than Arnold and informally, in his remarks in passing in letters, a more piercing critic, is more generous:

> When one reads Pope's Homer with a critical eye one sees, artificial as it is, in every couplet that he was a great man, but no doubt to an uncritical humour and an uncritical flippant modernist it does offer a great handle.

I now turn to the critical defenders of Pope. Before doing so, I would like to claim against Warton and Bowles, accepting their stiff and narrow prescriptive definition of poetry, and, against Arnold, accepting his tactfully vague and elastic one, that Pope is a great poet *on their own terms*. If Warton wants the pathetic and the sublime, I would refer him *Eloisa to Abelard, The Unfortunate Lady*, the passage on man on 'the dark isthmus of a middle state' in *An Essay on Man*, and the crashingly powerful conclusion of *The Dunciad*. To Bowles, if he is seeking for beauty in nature rather than art, I would offer the vivid colouring of the carp and the pheasant in *Windsor Forest*. Against Arnold, I would cite his own admission that Pope does the grand passages in Homer better than the flat passages and would recommend him to look again, and more alertly, for 'poetic largeness, freedom, insight, benignity'; largeness, once more, in that famous passage on man's paradoxical nature in *An Essay on Man*; freedom in the swift and natural transitions of mood in such a poem as the *Epistle to Dr Arbuthnot;* insight (poetic insight) in a hundred sketches of character from Atticus to Chloe; benignity as a general delight in friendship and a warmth that asserts itself against what his mind sees all too clearly as in the second sketch of Bolingbroke.Without (for the moment) attacking their principles, one can accuse all these critics of lazy and inattentive reading of their texts.

This is not, however, the only possible line of defence. The attack was on the pattern: 'Poetry is X. Pope's poems are not X. So Pope is not a poet.' Instead of questioning the minor premise, of asserting that Pope is at least at times X, as I have been doing, one can, like Dr Johnson, deny the major. What reason have we to assert dogmatically that poetry is X? Johnson writes:

> After all this, it is surely superfluous to answer the question that has once been asked, whether Pope was a poet, otherwise than by

asking, in return, if Pope be not a poet, where is poetry to be found? To circumscribe poetry by a definition will only show the narrowness of the definer, though a definition which shall exclude Pope will not easily be made.

Byron and Ruskin, Pope's great defenders in the nineteenth century, made what Pope had been most reproached with, his dealing with the moral problems of an artificial and complex society, the foundation of his praise. It is, after all, in such a society that we live. Can a poet be blamed for making his central subject the real problems of the world? Byron writes:

> He is the moral poet of all civilization; and as such, let us hope that he will one day be the national poet of mankind. He is the only poet that never shocks; the only poet whose faultlessness has been made his reproach . . . If his great charm be his melody, how comes it that foreigners adore him even in their diluted translations?

Part of Byron's defence is, of course, chivalrous nonsense. Pope, as in the character of Sporus in the *Epistle to Dr Arbuthnot*, often does intend to shock. He can be wantonly malignant as well as benign. 'The meanest passage is the satire on Sporus', wrote Dr Johnson, still today Pope's soundest critic: Johnson meant base or ignoble but our modern senses of 'mean', ungenerous, spiteful, may have been creeping in upon the word. Nor is Pope either morally or technically a 'faultless' poet. There is sometimes a painful contrast between the feelings which the rhetoric indicates and what we can guess, from the wider context, Pope's true feelings to have been. Too often Pope expresses what he knows he ought to feel, and does not; and the note is then forced.

Yet Ruskin, an admirer of Byron, but a man of temperament as different as one can imagine, shares, more soberly, this moral admiration:

> . . . the serene and just benevolence which placed Pope, in his theology, two centuries in advance of his time, and enabled him to sum the law of the noble life in two lines which, so far as I know, are the most complete, the most concise, and the most lofty expression of moral temper existing in English words –
> Never elated, while one man's oppressed;
> Never dejected, while another's blessed . . .

I wish you also to remember these lines of Pope, and to make

yourselves entirely masters of his system of ethics; because,
putting Shakespeare aside as rather the world's than ours, I hold
Pope to be the most perfect representative we have, since
Chaucer, of the true English mind; and I think *The Dunciad* the
most absolutely chiselled and monumental work 'exacted' in
our country.

It must be admitted that both Byron and Ruskin speak with a certain
conscious defiance, as if aware that the tide were turning against them;
also, that the moralising couplet Ruskin admires so much is an example
of what Arnold would call 'the application of ideas' to life rather than
'the *poetic* application of ideas'. It has a smug ring, Long before Arnold,
Blake, with his wonderfully delicate lyrical ear in short poems (I do
not find the same music, except at the beginning, in a work like *The
Book of Thel*, in the long monotonous lines of the Prophetic Books),   𝖷
had decided that the Popeian heroic couplet, with its tendency to a
see-saw movement and a mechanical break in the middle, was merely
ludicrous. He takes off Pope, as he hears him, in four lines scribbled in
a notebook whose contents date between 1808 and 1811:

Wondrous the gods, more wondrous are the men,
More wondrous, wondrous still, the cock, and hen,
More wondrous still the table, stool and chair;
But ah! more wondrous still the charming fair.

This is singularly unfair. It is funny because it is vapid and Pope is
always packed with sense, It is funny because its formal inanities are
addressed to nobody where Pope buttonholes the reader, as he buttonholes the character he is addressing in his poem. Still, Blake illustrates
what Cowper meant when he wrote about Pope:

Then, Pope, as harmony itself exact,
In verse well disciplined, complete, compact,
Gave virtue and morality a grace,
That quite eclipsing pleasure's painted face,
Levied a tax of wonder and applause
Even on fools that trampled on their laws,
But he – his musical finesse was such,
So nice his ear, so delicate his touch –
Made poetry a mere mechanic art,
And every warbler has his tune by heart.

Pope always wrote to rule and model. Blake never; had the two great men flourished in the same age and collided they would have hated each other, rightly, on instinct. Yet when Blake writes: 'I do not condemn Pope or Dryden because they did not understand imagination, but because they did not understand verse' – Blake cannot have read much Dryden or known of how many forms he was master besides the couplet – one wonders whether in the realm of 'imagination', which is not in dispute, the author of 'London' in *Songs of Experience* and the author of the darker passages of *The Dunciad* have not an uncomfortable deal in common. There is some region of horror and pity at which contrary imaginations meet.

For all the attacks on him, from his own day to ours, Pope's reputation will never be eclipsed. He is the central figure in one English tradition, which began with Denham and Waller, branched out with copious and uneven vigour in Dryden, speaks with concentrated, abrupt bitterness in Rochester, finds its richest variety in Pope himself, and leaves him three successors, none equalling him for polished modulation, but each excelling him in a single respect: Johnson in moral weight, Goldsmith in sweetness of sound and sentiment, Crabbe in the accurate representation of common life where there is no false glitter to hide its bareness and monotony. Of these three poets, Johnson, because of his power of thought, is probably the greatest. He is certainly even today, which is a great period of Pope scholarship, the greatest of Pope's critics. The Augustan tradition really came to an end with Crabbe, though Dr Leavis sees the Byron of *Beppo*, *The Vision of Judgment*, and *Don Juan* as, substituting his rapid *ottava rima* stanzas for the judgmental vigour and gravity of the couplet, and no longer really sure of his own standards, providing a kind of brilliant comic opera version of Augustan moral seriousness. If any single critic can be thought of as succeeding in putting Pope near the centre again it is Dr Leavis with his perceptively ranging chapter in *Revaluation* and his crisp and witty essay on *The Dunciad* in *The Common Pursuit*. Earlier on, critics for whom Dr Leavis could have little respect, Lytton Strachey in a Leslie Stephen lecture, Edith Sitwell in her unscholarly but readable study, *Alexander Pope* (1930), had made ineffective efforts to restore him to favour. Strachey's Pope is a crude caricature, a malignant monkey; interested only in sound, hardly at all in sense. Miss Sitwell creates her own Pope, only coincidentally similar at times to the real one.

There is no major poet in the English tradition so full of 'delicacies', subtleties of literary allusion and topical reference, as Pope. Swift, from Ireland, complained that he (and other writers of the time) made points incomprehensible to anybody living twenty miles out of London. He was also a great reviser, in successive reprintings, of what he had written, though not quite to the degree of Yeats. He has therefore in our own day attracted the scholars and the great Twickenham Edition, by various hands, which began to appear in 1939, and was completed with the addition of Pope's Homer in 1967, after it, has been one of the great works of critical editing of our time, ranking with Professor Kinsley's editions of Dryden and Burns, and the Cambridge and Arden Shakespeares. As an apparatus for the research student, it has assured Pope of continual attention in universities. But it is doubtful whether Pope is ever likely to regain wide popularity.

This is an age when satire in prose, like Evelyn Waugh's or Kingsley Amis's, is popular, and when the Australian Clive James even writes satire in verse. But there are no 'delicacies' in modern satire; it is above all brutal and personal. Our age is too intellectually slothful and too morally rank to produce, or to appreciate widely, 'delicacies' like Pope's. To appreciate him properly requires a quite unusual range of historical and philosophical curiosity and knowledge. Paradoxically, no English poet has written so clearly; none is harder either to expound or judge.

Yet can we not recognise in Pope three qualities that are out of fashion but that, if they could be miraculously restored to fashion, might improve our world? He is the great English poet of reason, virtue, and friendship. This, of course, itself sets up a barrier. Freud has taught us to mistrust reason (where it would explain to us our own motives) as mere 'rationalisation', a socially acceptable justification of our compulsive unconscious drives. Pope approved of reasonable self-love which by degrees, to fulfil itself properly, would develop by natural stages into social love and religious reverence. In this picture, Freud would see merely a smug disguise for the ego battered from above by the punishing super-ego and battered below by, but just managing to hold down, the insatiable id. (I realise that Freud is probably as out of date for many of my readers as Pope is, but he captivated my youth, and I do not think he has had any successors of the same stature.) On the whole, I am on Pope's side rather than Freud's. Freud said what he had to say about religion in *The Future of an Illusion*; Pope in *An Essay on Man*.

Pope believed in a benevolent God, a harmonious cosmos encouraging harmony among men, the basic naturalness and workableness into harmony of the human appetites and passions. He saw our ruling passions, our central obsessions, as working out for our good. Given all Pope's handicaps, of steady pain and ready resentment, would a man of equal genius, trained in Freudian pessimism and distrust of the checking power of reason, have lived a life in which suffering and distress were interspersed with so much happiness, a life so creatively productive? Critics of Pope, exulting in gross good health and the insensitivity that so often goes with that, have too often gloated over Pope's deviousness and petty vices; they have had little to say about the fiery and heroic spirit that led him so triumphantly through that 'long disease, my life'; or of his loving piety towards his parents; or of his loyalty towards the religion of his father and mother, however 'Erasmian' – humanist, latitudinarian, ecumenical – his own Roman Catholicism was. I do not blame him for religious insincerity because he lacked any of the zeal of the Spanish or Portuguese Inquisitions. God, I hope, will forgive him for being more humane than some of his co-religionists.

We do not boast of virtue, now – our own, or that of our friends. The fashion of new Grub Street and its various scandal sheets is to assume, as beyond argument, that every apparent virtue is a mask for corrupt private interests. Are we therefore better or more honest men? And, in fact, are the very deeply wicked and corrupt (if they have friends in high places) ever attacked as savagely as Pope attacked Colonel Francis Chartres?

As well as the poet of reason and virtue, I described Pope as the great poet of friendship. We find it hard today (and I speak for myself as much as for my readers, whom I do not assume to be worse and hope may be better men than myself) to believe in true friendship. Between men, friendship is often thought of as a mask to disguise rivalry and a socially inconvenient dislike. To be ready to sacrifice one's own interests for those of a friend is often thought a mark of weak sentimentality. We think it wise to trust nobody utterly (Pope would have been wise not to trust Bolingbroke utterly, but I should have thought the worse of him). At a level lower than that of intimate friendship, we are perhaps a little surprised if a colleague, having the power to make us look foolish, refrains from doing so. I speak of friendship between men: I agree with Byron that friendship between a man and a woman – so long as there is no question of sexual motives, though there may be any amount of liking for a physical presence, on either side – is the most delightful kind of friendship. There is nothing to compete about in such a friendship; it can be perfectly easy, whereas in even the best and loyalest friendships between men there is nearly always just a touch of latent aggressiveness on either side. But both kinds of friendship (Pope and Swift, or Pope and Martha Blount) enormously enrich life. One will not die happier for reflecting that one has never, out of spontaneous affection or sheer admiration, put oneself in the power of anybody.

Pope, no more than the rest of us, lived a wholly virtuous life, a consistently reasonable one, one of absolutely loyal friendship (one thinks again of the brilliant portrait in *Of the Characters of Women*, and all it implies of spite and ingratitude, of Henrietta Howard). But he is the only English poet who has preached reason, virtue, and friendship from the beginning, and from the heart. That, with his brilliant art in verse, makes him a classic: a specially improving one for our own age.

Select Bibliography

1 Poems and other works published in Pope's lifetime and, under Warburton's care, shortly after his death

1709 *The Pastorals*, in the sixth part of Tonson's *Miscellanies*.
1711 *An Essay on Criticism*.
1712 *Messiah*, in *The Spectator*. First version of *The Rape of the Lock* in Lintot's *Miscellany*.
1713 *Windsor Forest*.
1714 Enlarged version of *The Rape of the Lock*.
1715 *The Temple of Fame*.
      The Iliad, Books I–IV.
1716 The *Iliad*, vol. II.
1717 The *Iliad*, vol. III.
      Pope's *Works*, including first publication of *Verses to the Memory of an Unfortunate Lady* and *Eloisa to Abelard*.
1718 The *Iliad*, vol. IV.
1720 The *Iliad*, vols V and VI.
1721 *Epistle to Addison*, prefaced to Tickell's edition of Addison's works.
      Epistle to Oxford, prefaced to Pope's edition of Parnell's poems.
1723 Pope's edition, at the Duchess's request, of the *Works* of John Sheffield, Duke of Buckingham. Political repercussions because of Jacobite strain in the late Duke's poems.
1725 Edition of Shakespeare in six volumes.
      Odyssey, vols I–III, with assistance of Fenton and Broome.
1726 *Odyssey*, vols IV–V.
1727 Pope–Swift *Miscellanies*, vols I and II.
1728 Pope–Swift *Miscellanies*, 'last' volume, including *Peri Bathous* or *The Art of Sinking in Poetry*.
      The Dunciad (in three books).
1729 The *Dunciad Variorum*.
1732 *Epistle to Burlington* (Moral Essay IV).

1732 Pope–Swift *Miscellanies*, 'third' volume.
1733 *Epistle to Bathurst* (Moral Essay III).
 The first *Imitation of Horace* (Satires II i).
 An Essay on Man, Epistles I to III (anonymous).
1734 *Epistle to Cobham* (Moral Essay I).
 An Essay on Man, Epistle IV.
 Imitation of Horace (Satires II ii).
 Sober Advice from Horace (improper and very funny, never officially acknowledged by Pope.
1735 *Epistle to Dr Arbuthnot*.
 Of the Characters of Women (an epistle to Martha Blount who is, however, not named). (Moral Essay II).
 Pope's *Works*, Vol. II.
 Curl's edition of Pope's letters.
1737 *Imitations of Horace* (Epistles II i).
 Imitations of Horace (Epistles II ii).
1738 *Imitations of Horace* (Epistles I vi and I i).
1742 *The New Dunciad* (Book IV).
1743 *The Dunciad* in four books, with Cibber replacing Theobald as the hero.
1744 Pope's death.
1751 Pope's *Works* in nine volumes, edited by William Warburton.

2 Important later editions

The standard modern edition is *The Twickenham Edition of the Poems of Alexander Pope*, whose general editor was the late John Butt, 11 vols, London and New Haven, 1939–69.

I *Pastoral Poetry and an Essay on Criticism*, ed. E. Audra and Aubrey Williams, 1961.
II *The Rape of the Lock and Other Poems*, ed. Geoffrey Tillotson, 3rd edn. 1962.
III.i *An Essay on Man*, ed. Maynard Mack, 1950.
III.ii *Epistles to Several Persons (Moral Essays)*, ed. F. W. Bateson, 2nd edn. 1961.
IV *Imitations of Horace, with An Epistle to Dr Arbuthnot and the Epilogue to the Satires*, ed. John Butt, 2nd edn. 1953.
V *The Dunciad*, ed., James Sutherland, 3rd edn. 1953.
VI *Minor Poems*, ed. Norman Ault and John Butt, 1954.
VII, VIII: *The Iliad of Homer*; IX, X: *The Odyssey of Homer*, ed. Maynard Mack, with Norman Callan, Robert Fagles, William Frost and Douglas M. Knight, 1967.
XI *Index*, ed. Maynard Mack, 1969.
A condensed version of this, without Homer, without the introductions to separate volumes, and with a necessarily drastic reduction of the annotations,

is: *The Poems of Alexander Pope; A One-Volume Edition of the Twickenham Text with Selected Annotations*, ed. John Butt, 1963.

The most reliable earlier edition, in spite of the hostile attitude of the editors to Pope as a man, is *The Works of Alexander Pope*, ed. Whitwell Elwin and W. J. Courthope, 10 vols, 1871-89.

3 Prose works and memorabilia

The Correspondence of Alexander Pope, ed. George Sherburn, 5 vols, Oxford, 1956.
Letters of Alexander Pope, ed. John Butt, 1960. A selection.
The Prose Works of Alexander Pope, ed. Norman Ault, vol 1, *The Earlier Works, 1711-1720*, Oxford 1936. To be completed by Maynard Mack.
The Art of Sinking in Poetry: Martinus Scriblerus, Peri Bathous, ed. Edna Leake Steeves, New York, 1952.
Memoirs of the Extraordinary Life, Works, and Discoveries of Martinus Scriblerus, ed. Charles Kerby-Miller, New Haven, 1950.
The Literary Criticism of Alexander Pope, ed. Bertrand A. Goldgar, Lincoln, Nebraska, 1965.
Spence, Joseph, *Observations, Anecdotes, and Characters of Books and Men*, ed. James M. Osborn, 2 vols, Oxford, 1966.

4 Bibliographies and a concordance

Abbott, Edwin, *A Concordance to the Works of Pope*, based on Warburton's edition of 1751.
Griffith, R. H., *Alexander Pope: A Bibliography*, vol. I, *Pope's Own Writings*, two parts, Austin, Texas, 1922-7, discontinued.
Lopez, Cecilia L., *Alexander Pope: An Annotated Bibliography, 1945-67*, Florida, 1970. A bibliography of critical and scholarly studies over the period stated.
Tobin, James E., *Alexander Pope: a list of Critical Studies published from 1895 to 1944*, New York, 1948.
Abbot, Edwin, *A Concordance to the Works of Pope*, New York, 1875. Based on Warburton's edition of 1751.

5 Biographies, some partly critical

Ruffhead, Owen, *The Life of Alexander Pope*, London, 1769.
Johnson, Samuel, *The Life of Pope*, in *Lives of the Poets*, London, 1781.
Sitwell, Edith, *Alexander Pope*, London, 1930.

Sherburn, George, *The Early Career of Alexander Pope*, Oxford, 1934.
Dobrée, Bonamy, *Alexander Pope*, London, 1951.
Quennell, Peter, *Alexander Pope: The Education of Genius, 1688–1728*. London, 1969.

6 Other relevant biographies

Dickinson, H. T., *Bolingbroke*, London, 1970.
Halsband, Robert, *Lord Hervey, Eighteenth-Century Courtier*, Oxford, 1973.

7 Selected critical studies

Arden, John M., *Something Like Horace: Studies in the Art and Allusion of Pope's Horatian Satires*. Nashville, Tennessee, 1969.
Bateson, F. W. and Joukovsky, N. A. (eds), *Alexander Pope: A Critical Anthology*, Harmondsworth, 1971.
Brower, Reuben A., *Alexander Pope: The Poetry of Allusion*, Oxford, 1959.
Cunningham, J. S., *Pope: 'The Rape of the Lock'. Studies in English Literature*, London, 1961.
Dixon, Peter, *The World of Pope's Satires: An Introduction to the 'Epistles' and 'Imitations of Horace'*, London, 1968.
Empson, William, *Seven Types of Ambiguity*, 3rd edn, London, 1935, esp. pp. 70–4, 125–8, 149–51.
Empson, William, 'Wit in the *Essay on Criticism*', in *The Structure of Complex Words*, London, 1951.
Jack, Ian, *Augustan Satire: Intention and Idiom in English Poetry, 1660–1750*, Oxford, 1952. Especially chapters v to vii.
Wilson Knight, G., *Laureate of Peace; on the Genius of Alexander Pope*, London and New York, 1954.
Leavis, F. R., *Revaluation: Tradition and Development in English Poetry*, London, 1936.
Leavis, F. R., 'The Dunciad' in *The Common Pursuit*, London, 1952.
Mack, Maynard, *The Garden and the City: Retirement and Politics in the Later Poetry of Alexander Pope, 1731–43*, Toronto, 1969.
Mason, H. A., *To Homer through Pope: an Introduction to Homer's Iliad and Pope's Translation*, London, 1972.
Rogers, R. W., *The Major Satires of Alexander Pope*, Urbana, Illinois, 1955.
Tillotson, Geoffrey, *On the Poetry of Pope*, 2nd edn, Oxford, 1959.
Tillotson, Geoffrey, *Pope and Human Nature*, Oxford, 1958.
Trickett, Rachel, *The Honest Muse: A Study in Augustan Verse*, London, 1967.
Warren, Austin, *Alexander Pope as Critic and Humanist*, Princeton 1929.

Wimsatt, W. K., 'One Relation of Rhyme to Reason; Alexander Pope' and 'Rhetoric and Poems: Alexander Pope', both reprinted in *The Verbal Icon*, Kentucky, 1954, London, 1970.

Wimsatt, W. K., *The Portraits of Alexander Pope*, New Haven and London, 1965. (This last should perhaps come under biography, but Pope's portraits seem to illuminate his poetry more directly than the evasive annals of his life do.)

8 Background books

Humphreys, A. R., *The Augustan World: Life and Letters in Eighteenth-Century England*. London, 1954.

Lovejoy, A. O., *The Great Chain of Being: A Study of the History of an Idea*. Cambridge, Mass., 1936 (A modern classic and the creator of a new academic discipline. Specially relevant to Pope's *Essay on Man*.)

Plumb, J. H., *The Growth of Political Stability in England, 1675–1725*, London, 1967.

Walcott, Robert, *English Politics in the Early Eighteenth Century*, Oxford, 1956.

Watt, Ian (ed), *The Augustan Age: Approaches to its Literature, Life, and Thought*, Greenwich, Conn., 1968.

Williams, Basil, *The Whig Supremacy, 1714–1760*, 2nd edn, revised by C. H. Stuart, Oxford, 1962.

Wimsatt, William K., and Brooks, Cleanth, *Literary Criticism: A Short History*, New York and London, 1957.

9 Pope's visual world

Dixon Hunt, John, and Willis, Peter (eds), *The Genius of Place: The English Landscape Garden 1620–1820*, London, 1975.

Index